Don't Let the Pigeon Finish This Activity Book!

words by mo willems and mr. warburton

pictures by mo willems

HYPERION BOOKS FOR CHILDREN/New York

Hi! I'm the Bus Driver. Welcome to this activity book! Look for me at the bottom of each page, and I will tell you what you need for each activity!

Hi! I'm the Duckling! Are you ready to do some really fun activities?

Here I am!

And I'm the Pigeon. I am an expert at finishing activity books!

Use crayons to color the black-and-white pages (like this one)!

PERFORATED!

> # Hey there, grown-ups! I'm here to tell you about this activity book!

THINGS YOU SHOULD KNOW:

- A book can be read AND played. This book provides loads of opportunities for your kid to do both, alone or with you!

- This book is packed with activities both small and big. Some take up just a page, while others are multi-paged events!

- There is a narrative to this book, but if you want to skip around, go for it!

- Sure, we made these activities to be fun, but we took the extra step of having them all vetted by an early learning specialist. The activities cover a range of abilities, so be ready to help your child with some of the harder ones. Lucky you!

- Every page is perforated, so when your child is done, you can tear out their masterpiece and hang it up (or put it in one of the handy folders at the front or back of the book)!

- You'll find a solutions key at the end of the book!

- We use icons throughout the book in the band at the bottom of the page. Here's what they mean:

Use a pencil (or crayon) for activities that require you to draw or write!

You'll need a box of crayons for the drawing and coloring pages!

Have some tape handy!

Some activities ask you to cut things out — you'll need a pair of scissors. Make sure to help your child with the trickier shapes.

You might want extra pieces of paper for these activities.

A few activities require these special items: string; a stapler; and coins (or buttons or paper clips)—please keep a close eye on your kids when they're using these small objects.

> Well, that's about it. Let's get started!
> And whatever you do:
> don't let the Pigeon finish this activity book!

This book is dedicated to our kids, and yours

Words: **Mo Willems** and **Mr. Warburton**

Illustrations: **Mo Willems**

Book design and additional illustrations: **Scott Sosebee**

First Edition
15 14 13 12 11 10
FAC-039745-23020

FSC
www.fsc.org

MIX
Paper | Supporting
responsible forestry
FSC® C013572

Printed in South Korea

ISBN 978-1-4231-3310-0

Visit
www.hyperionbooksforchildren.com
and
www.pigeonpresents.com

Can we please get back to ME?

Now that we are done with all of that boring grown-up stuff ...

get a pencil and write your name on the line below.

YOUR NAME

You will need something to write with for this activity!

WE ARE DONE THIS ACTIVITY

HA!

YES!

YAY! Let's draw me!

1. Start with a big letter "O".
(It appears in words like "Mo"!)

2. Now, draw a smaller letter "O" inside of it.
(You've drawn a doughnut!)

3. Next, you have a choice between two letters — "M" or "W" — but draw the letter on its side.
(You made a beak!)

4. We're going to place the eye next, which is the most important part of the drawing, because the eye shows how the character is feeling. Make sure to darken it in.
(You always look at the darkest part of a drawing first!)

5. Draw two lines going straight down for the neck.

6. Next, draw two lines across the neck for the collar.

7. The body is a circ-angle, a triangle and a circle combined.
(It kind of looks like an ice cream cone that's fallen over.)

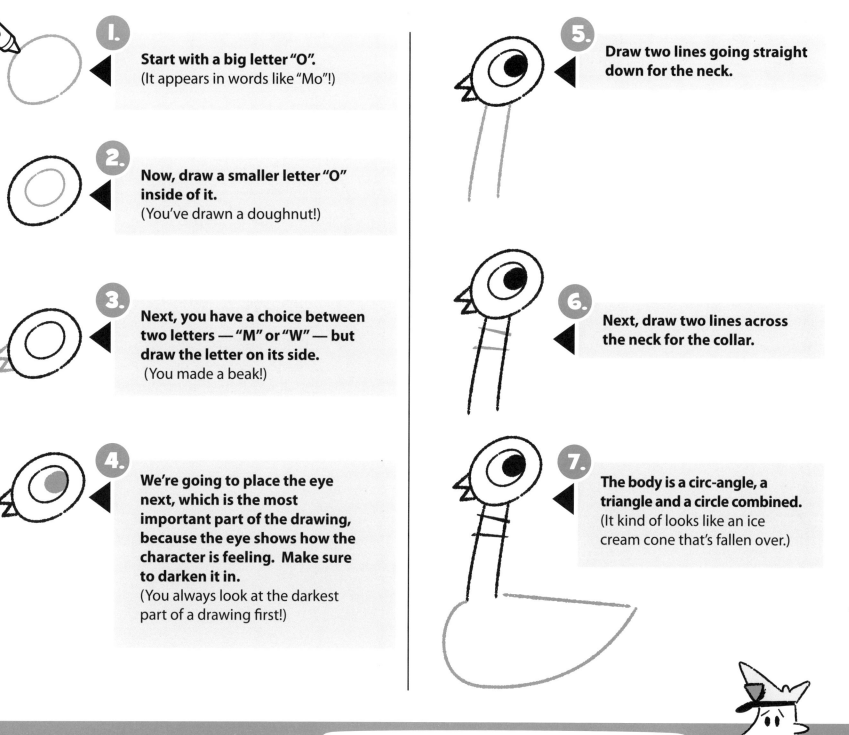

Turn the page for more instructions!

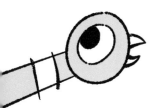

8.

◄ **The legs are two more lines straight down from the body.** (Just like the neck!)

FINISHED!

9.

◄ **Almost done! Draw the letter "V" three times. The first two are upside down for the feet. The third is on its side in the body for the wing.**

Great job! That's an awesome Pigeon!
Once you've gotten the basic drawing down, mix it up. Move his beak, his wings, his eye, and his legs to create lots of different poses and emotions!

Tear out this page and save it in one of the book's folders. You can practice drawing the Pigeon on the next page.

HEAD

NECK

BODY

LEGS

Trace the Pigeon on the left, then practice drawing the Pigeon on your own in the space provided.

HEAD

NECK

BODY

LEGS

Use these two pages to practice drawing the Pigeon.

HEAD

NECK

BODY

LEGS

If you want to practice even more, get some paper and start drawing!

15

That drawing you made of me **ROCKS!** Let's go hang it up in my house!

We can take the bus!

IT'S TIME FOR A
BIG ACTIVITY!

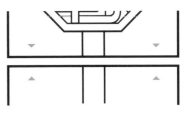

1 Pull the **next two pages** out of your activity book!

2 Lay them out on a table or on the floor. Make sure the white sides are facing UP!

3 Fit the pages together where the arrows indicate.

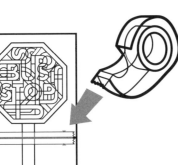

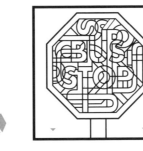

4 Tape the pages together!

5 Color in all of the shapes with blue dots to read the sign.

6 Hang up your sign on a wall and sit down next to it!

A "BIG ACTIVITY" is one for which you may need a grown-up to help. You'll need these things to do this activity.

TOSS-A-MA-BOB!

Anything that lands OUTSIDE the circle is worth 1 point!

The Pigeon sure looks happy! Draw something that makes you happy on one of these pages, then color them both!

 The bus door won't open until it's colored in! Once you finish, turn the page!

HELP! I'm being chased—

What are the Pigeon and Mad Cow running through? A field of grass? Mud? Coleslaw? You decide, and then draw it!

by a MAD COW!!!

Color in all the squares with Pigeon footprints (木木) to help him escape the Mad Cow!

32

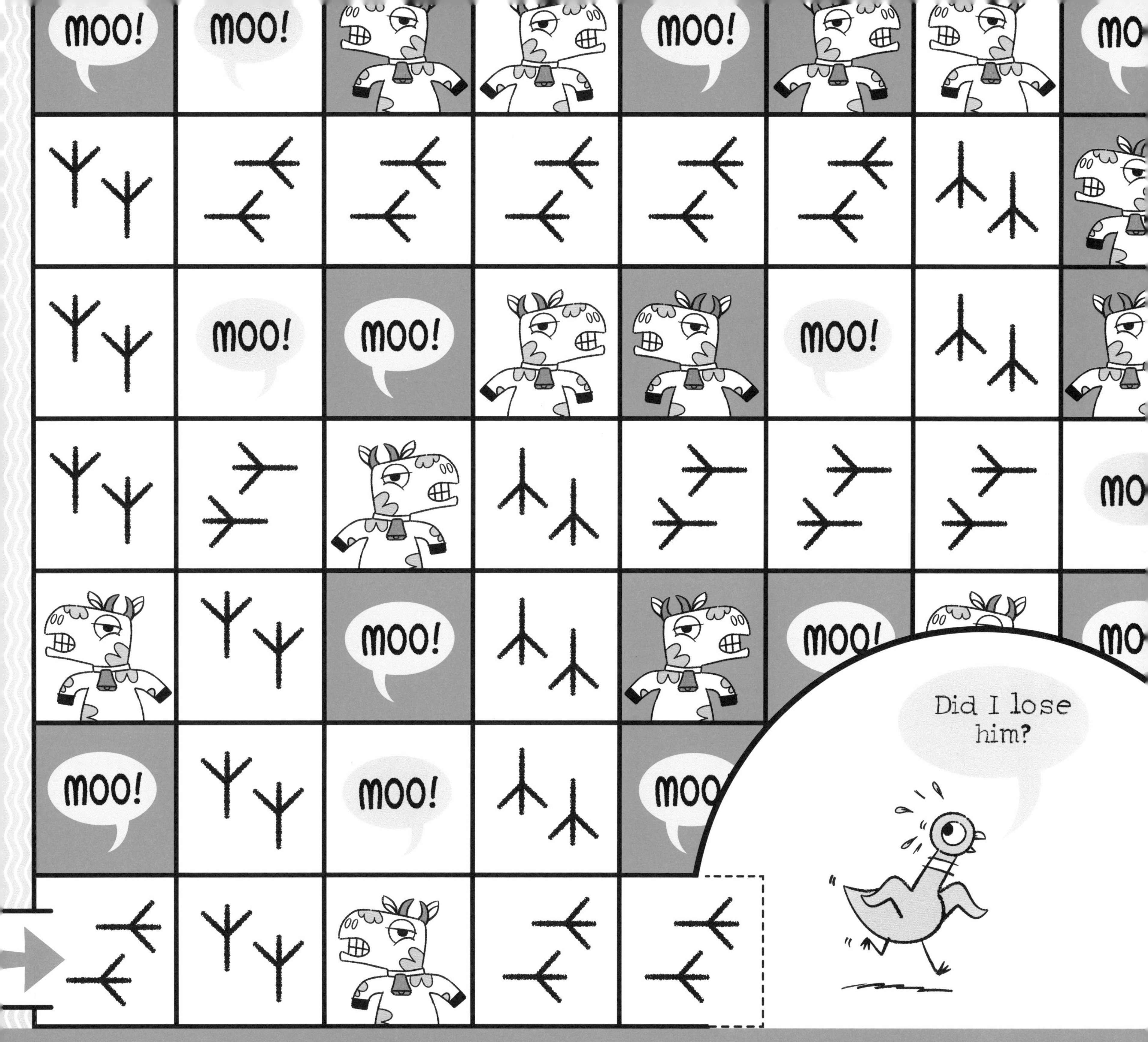
MOO!
Did I lose him?

What should we do while the Pigeon is busy playing with the Mad Cow?

The Duckling's idea sounds exciting. Draw as many exclamation points around her head as you can!

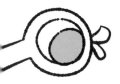

Let's play
Toss-a-Ma-Bob!

1 Take your bus stop off the wall.

2 Turn it over to magically reveal a Toss-a-Ma-Bob target!

3 Get three coins. (You can also use buttons.)

4 Place your Toss-a-Ma-Bob target on the ground.

5 Step away from the target. Not too close, but not too far.

6 Toss a coin at the target. If your coin lands completely within one of the circles, yell "Toss-a-Ma-Bob!"

7 Take turns tossing coins. The first person to reach 10 points is the winner!

To play the game, you'll need some coins or other small objects to toss!

There are lots of fun ways to play Toss-a-Ma-Bob!

If you're right-handed, try throwing the coins with your left hand; or with your right hand if you're a lefty!

Try playing with your eyes closed!

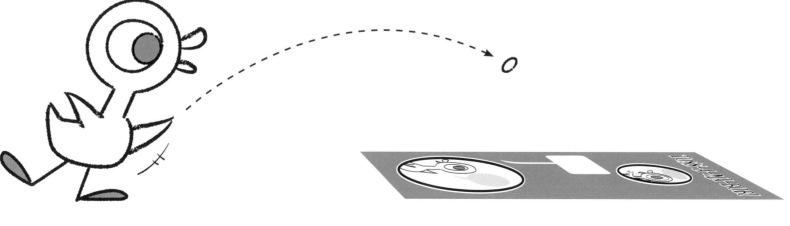

It's for you.

FROM:
The Pigeon

TO: _____
    NAME

    _____
    STREET

                    STATE
    _____
    CITY

Write your name and
address on the envelope!

A playdate with the Pigeon! I wonder what his house looks like!

 Draw what you think the Pigeon's house looks like!

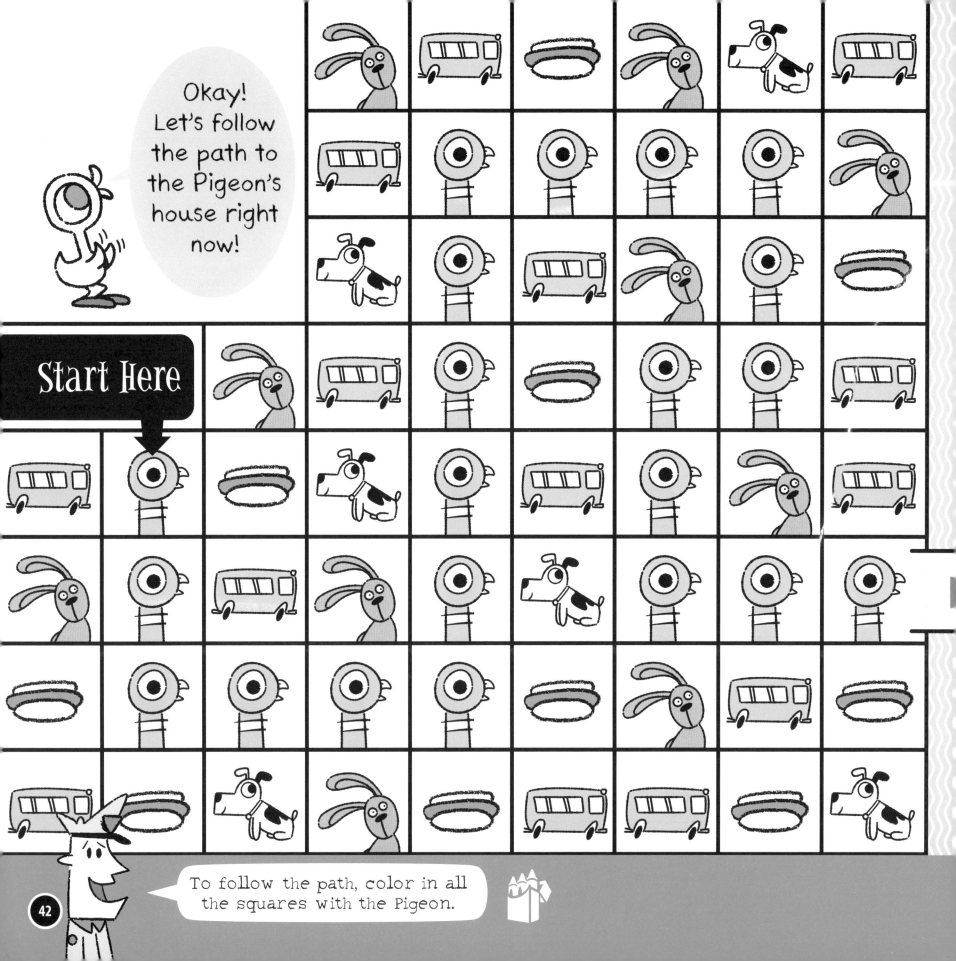

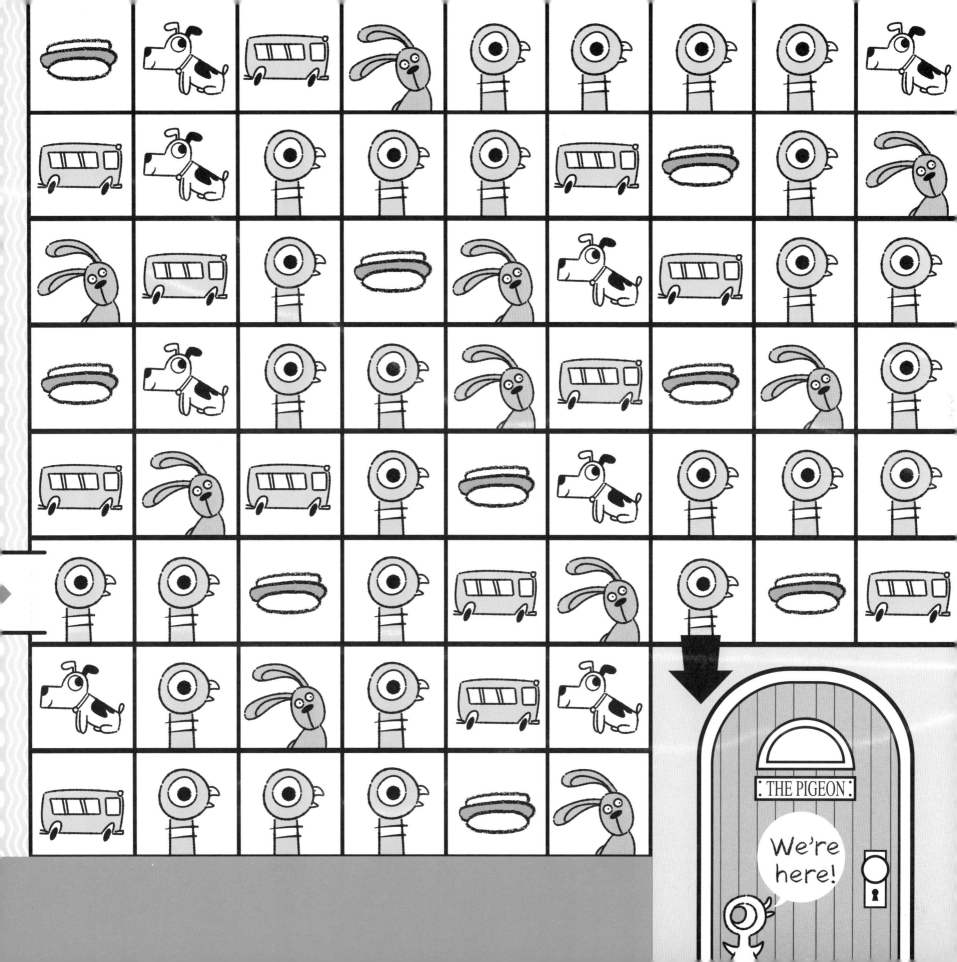

Let's make a knocker to put on the Pigeon's door!

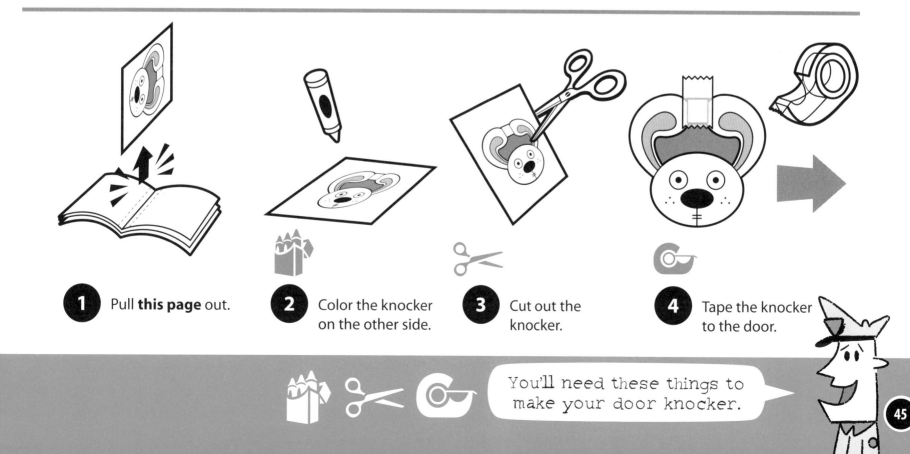

1 Pull **this page** out.

2 Color the knocker on the other side.

3 Cut out the knocker.

4 Tape the knocker to the door.

You'll need these things to make your door knocker.

Hey . . .
that door knocker
looks familiar!

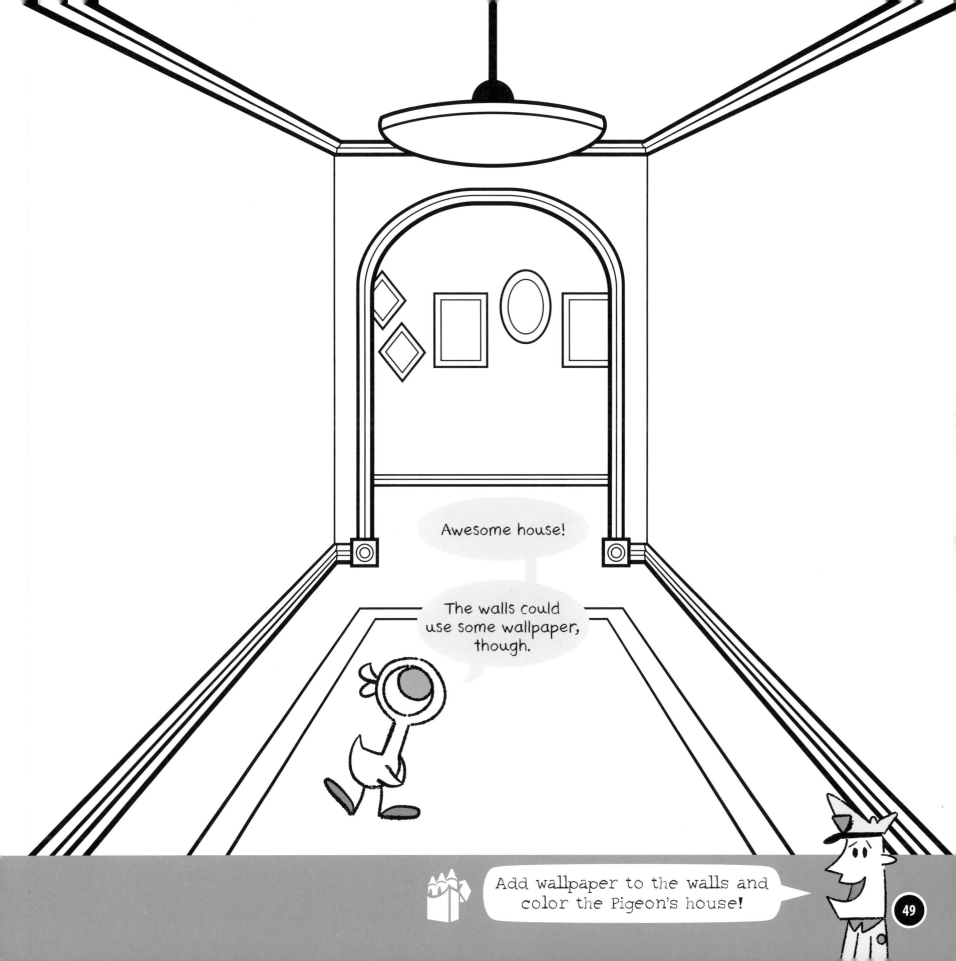

MARTY THE

COUSIN LASSO
FAMOUS COW WRANGLER

JUMBO
WORLD'S SMALLEST PIGEON

SIR PIGEON, THE BLUE KNIGHT

PAPA PIGEON'S FAVORITE HAT

More pictures and names are missing. Fill them in!

HOT DOG CHOMP!

BUS TV

TOYS

Color the Pigeon's stuff. Then turn the page to finish this activity.

1 Pull out **this page**.

2 Cut out the games and furniture.

3 Tape the pieces in the Pigeon's playroom!

OH, NO! What happened to all my stuff?

You can draw stuff in the Pigeon's playroom, too!

Make my playroom look cool!

You will need these things to do this activity.

Draw yourself sitting in between the Duckling and Pigeon.

The Duckling and Pigeon need a snack! Draw your favorite foods on this page!

Let's race to the kitchen!

Great idea!

1 Remove **this page** and the **next page**.

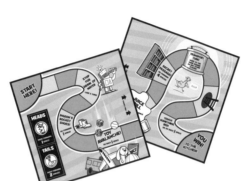 **2** Lay them flat with the blue side facing up.

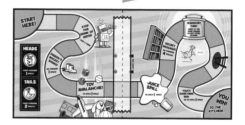 **3** Tape the pages together where the arrows indicate.

 **4** You and up to three more players each pick something to use as a game piece. It can be a button, a stamp, a paper clip, or even a torn piece of paper!

 **5** Place your piece on the game board where it reads "START HERE!"

 **6** Players take turns flipping the coin. If it's "heads," move forward one space. If it's "tails," move forward two spaces. Then follow the instructions on your square. First player to finish wins!

 For this activity, you will need tape, something to use as game pieces, and a coin.

Who won the race to the kitchen? Draw yourself and the other players on the winners' stand.

O B
U C

THE
PIGEON
WANTS
A
SNACK

QUICK! Make up a password and put it on the fridge!

Y

You can also make silly words, like "PANTSY."

WRITE YOUR OWN LETTERS IN THE BLANK BOXES ABOVE.

Color the letters, cut them out, and then tape them to the Pigeon's refrigerator to spell funny things!

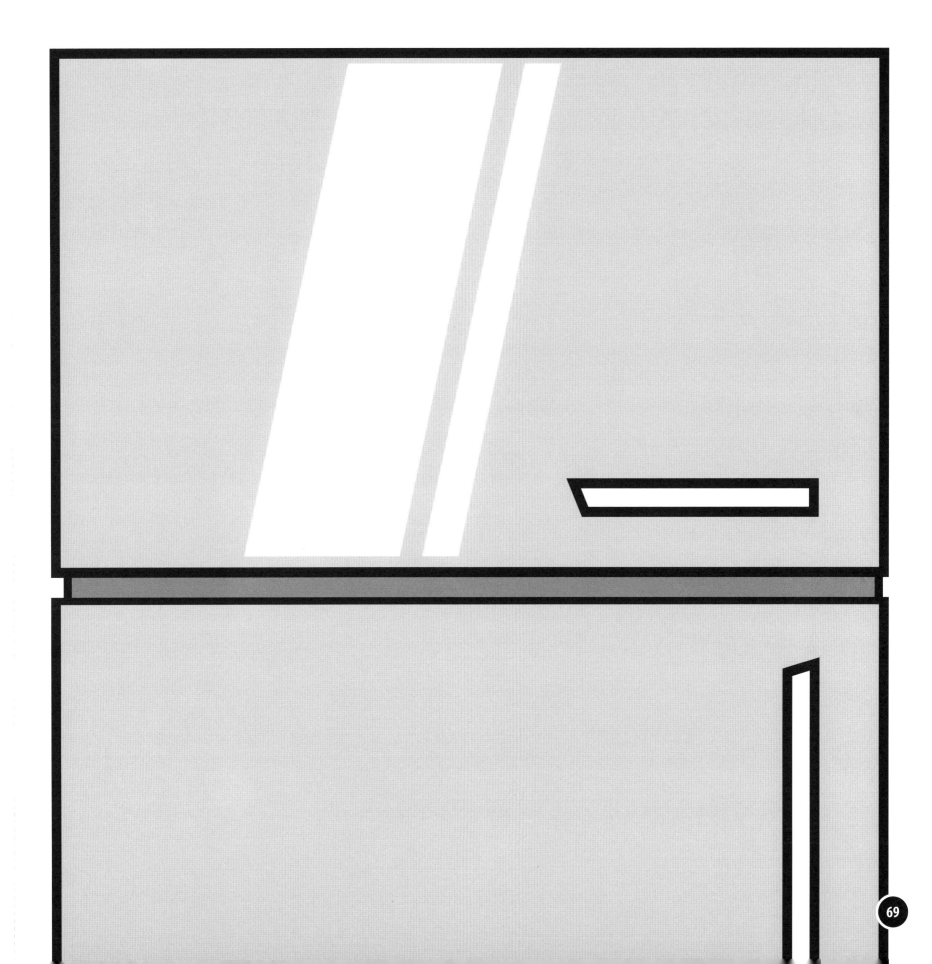

Draw all types of food in the Pigeon's fridge!

71

LATER...

The Pigeon ate so much, he's seeing spots! Fill the page with spots of different colors and sizes!

The Pigeon sure is excited! Draw lightning all around him, and then color this page!

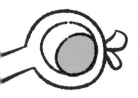
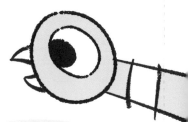

It's time for another
BIG ACTIVITY!
Let's make a picture book!

Hooray! I'll be a star!

1 Tear out the **next six pages** of the book.

2 Follow the directions on each page by filling in the blanks and adding illustrations.

3 Once you're done, stack the pages. Make sure they're in the right order!

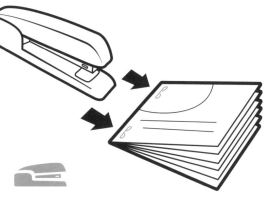

4 Staple twice at the edge where indicated.

You'll need these things for this activity. And if you need help, ask a grown-up!

Let's Let the Pigeon

_____ **!**

Finally!

DRAW YOURSELF HERE.

DRAW THE PIGEON HERE.

words and pictures by _____

Hi, my name is

_____.

I'm going to leave for
a little while. Can you
make sure to let the
Pigeon

_____

_____?

DRAW YOURSELF HERE.

Hi! Can I _____

_____ ?

DRAW WHAT YOU'LL LET THE PIGEON DO HERE.

DRAW THE PIGEON'S LEGS DANCING. THE MORE LEGS YOU DRAW THE BETTER!

Hmmm . . . I wonder if the Pigeon is having fun?

DRAW YOURSELF SITTING AT THE TABLE. (DON'T FORGET TO DRAW YOUR LUNCH!)

Phew! I think I'll take a break and have a cup of _____ before I _____ _____ again.

HEY! Come back with my

!

DRAW THE MAD COW HOLDING WHAT HE TOOK FROM THE PIGEON.

DRAW YOURSELF HERE.

THE AUTHOR

DRAW YOUR PICTURE IN THE FRAME.

The author is
_____ years old
and likes books
about

_____

_____

_____

and wants to

_____

_____

_____

and lives in

_____

_____ !

01011100

Published by Pigeon Press
Rat With Wings Blvd.
Coo York, NY oxoxox

Wow!
You just finished
your very own
picture
book!

  Color the Duckling and then draw confetti all around her!

Color your medal with all of your favorite colors. Then, cut it out and tape it to your chest. You earned it!

Tear out this page! You'll use these things to make your medal.

89

If you think I'm a better author, you can use this side of the medal!

This is the back of your medal!

A BOOK SIGNING?
I LOVE BOOK SIGNINGS!!!

I better start practicing my autograph!

Draw hearts all over the page!

Here are some autographs by famous people! Practice writing your name in their style, and then your own!

Walt Disney

⅄ Pigeon ⅄

Mo!

_____

_____

_____

YOUR NAME ➤ _____

YOUR NAME ➤ _____

YOUR NAME ➤ _____

Once you're done, tear this page out. Turn it over, draw yourself, and then tape it up where everyone can see it!

Hey, what's that you're holding?

It's a microphone. We need one to read our book out loud at the book signing!

You can make one, too!

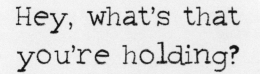

Draw question marks all over the page!

It's time for another
BIG ACTIVITY!

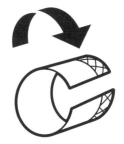

1 Remove the **next page** from the book.

2 Color both sides of your microphone.

3 Roll the microphone page into a tube.

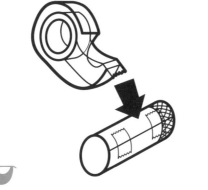

4 Place two small pieces of tape where indicated.

5 Your microphone is finished!

You'll need these things to make your microphone.

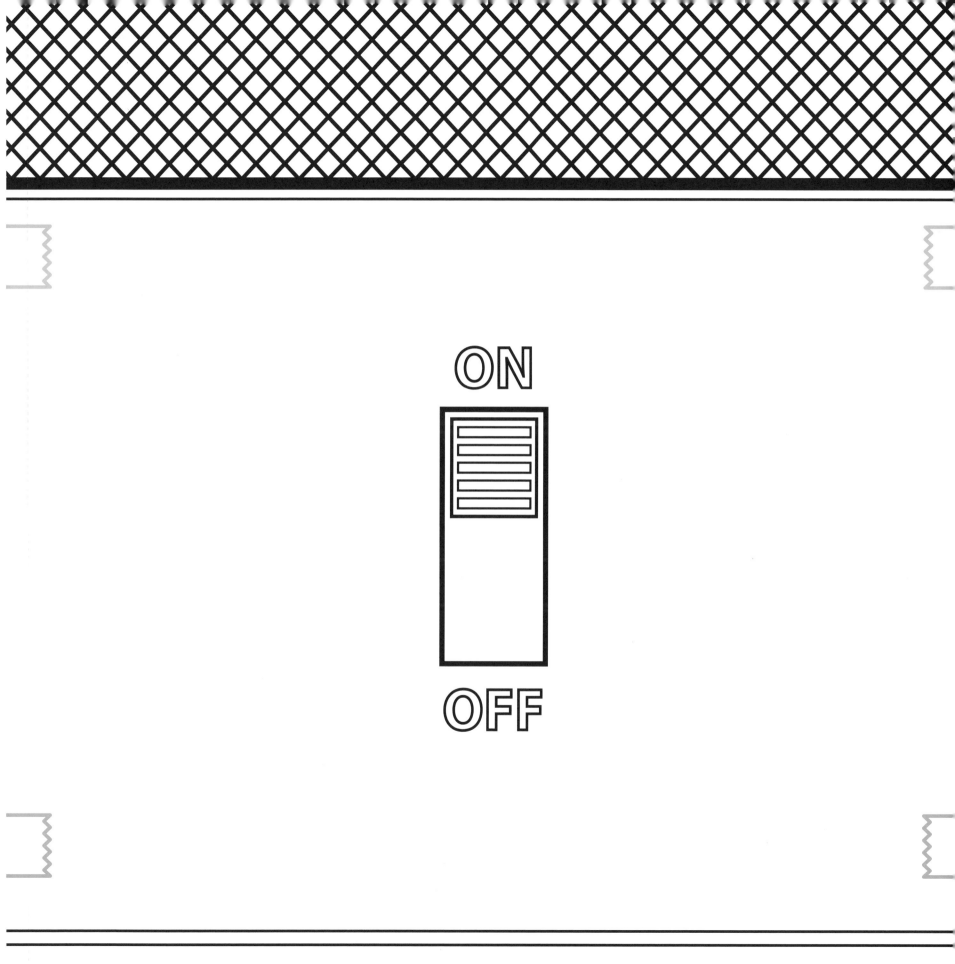

This is the inside of your microphone. Color the batteries!

THIS CARD ENTITLES THE OWNER TO
ONE FREE AUTOGRAPH
FROM THE AUTHOR OF
BOOK TITLE

THIS CARD ENTITLES THE OWNER TO
ONE FREE AUTOGRAPH
FROM THE AUTHOR OF
BOOK TITLE

THIS CARD ENTITLES THE OWNER TO
ONE FREE AUTOGRAPH
FROM THE AUTHOR OF
BOOK TITLE

THIS CARD ENTITLES THE OWNER TO
ONE FREE AUTOGRAPH
FROM THE AUTHOR OF
BOOK TITLE

THIS CARD ENTITLES THE OWNER TO
ONE FREE AUTOGRAPH
FROM THE AUTHOR OF
BOOK TITLE

THIS CARD ENTITLES THE OWNER TO
ONE FREE AUTOGRAPH
FROM THE AUTHOR OF
BOOK TITLE

Tear out this page and then cut out the six postcards.
Make sure to bring them to your book signing!

THANKS FOR COMING TO MY BOOK SIGNING!

YOUR AUTOGRAPH

THANKS FOR COMING TO MY BOOK SIGNING!

YOUR AUTOGRAPH

THANKS FOR COMING TO MY BOOK SIGNING!

YOUR AUTOGRAPH

THANKS FOR COMING TO MY BOOK SIGNING!

YOUR AUTOGRAPH

THANKS FOR COMING TO MY BOOK SIGNING!

YOUR AUTOGRAPH

THANKS FOR COMING TO MY BOOK SIGNING!

YOUR AUTOGRAPH

This is the other side of your postcards!

LATER ...

Wow!
That book signing was a
great way to finish this
activity book!

We can't stop
now! We're late
for the puppet
show!

Color each of the stripes around the Pigeon's head a different color.

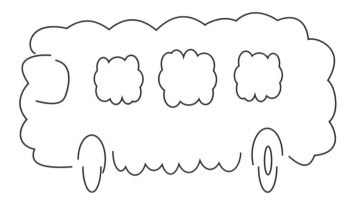

107

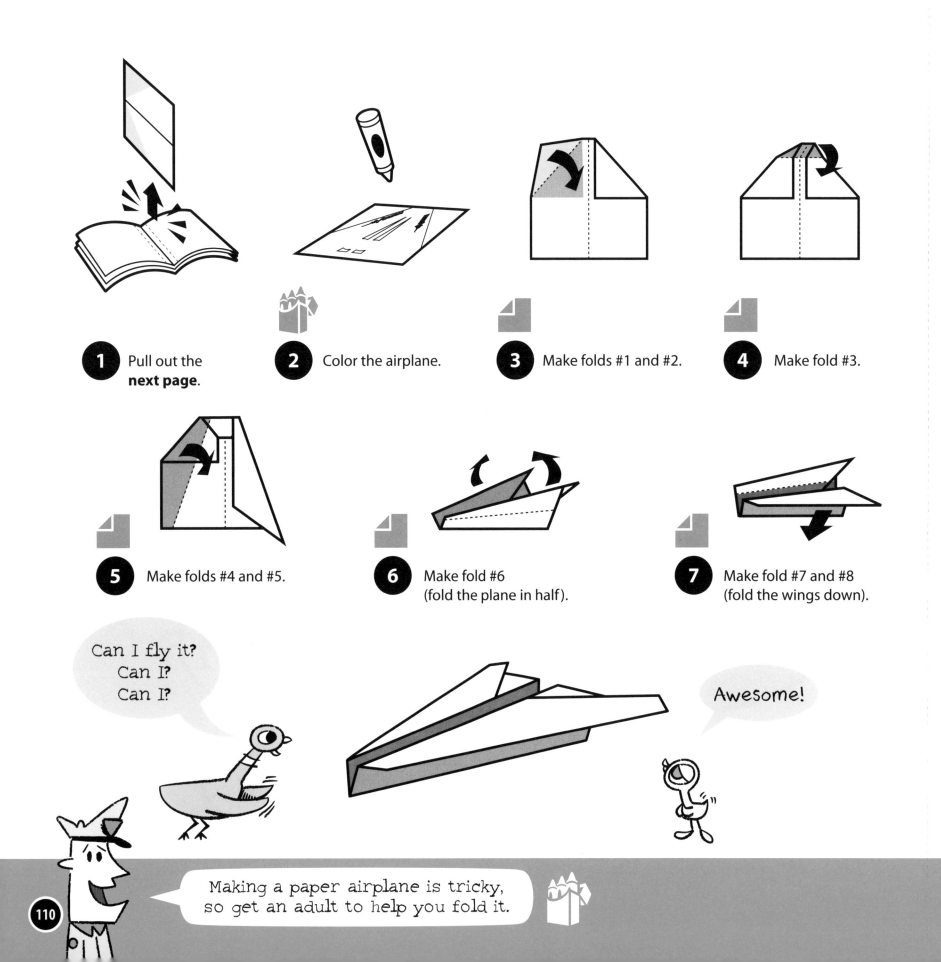

1 Pull out the **next page**.

2 Color the airplane.

3 Make folds #1 and #2.

4 Make fold #3.

5 Make folds #4 and #5.

6 Make fold #6 (fold the plane in half).

7 Make fold #7 and #8 (fold the wings down).

Can I fly it? Can I? Can I?

Awesome!

Making a paper airplane is tricky, so get an adult to help you fold it.

110

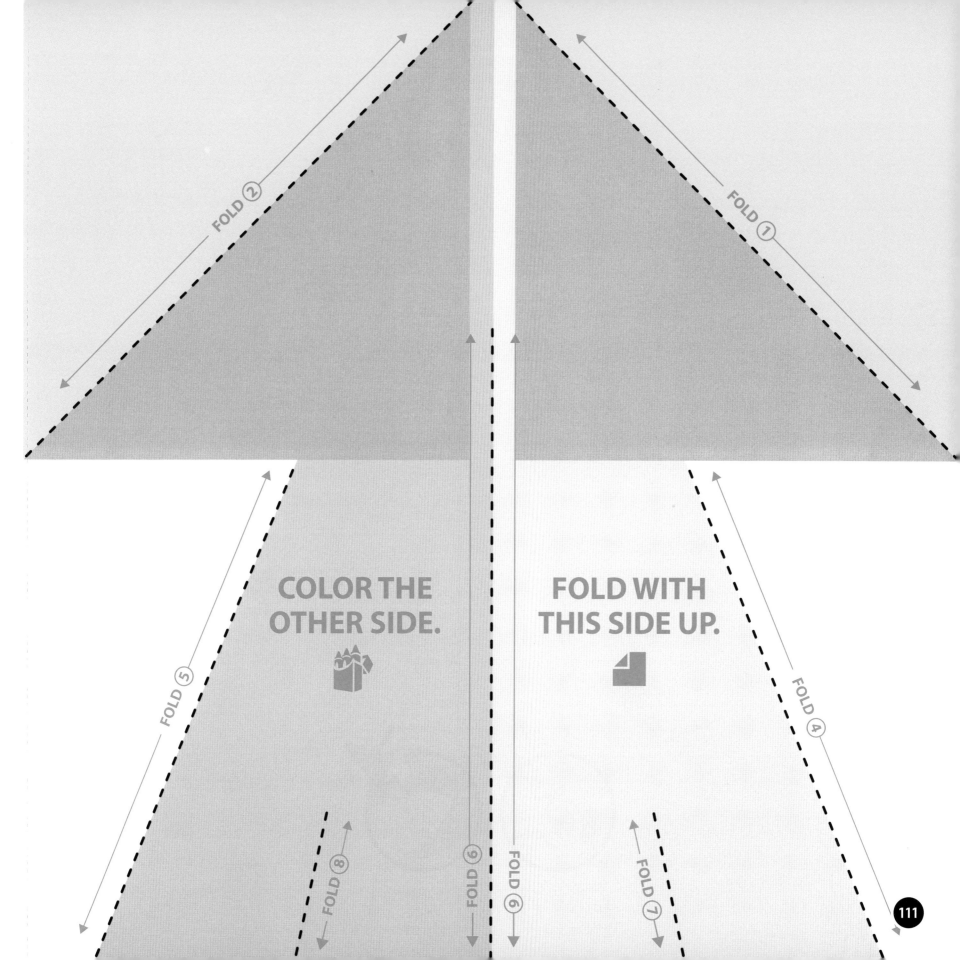

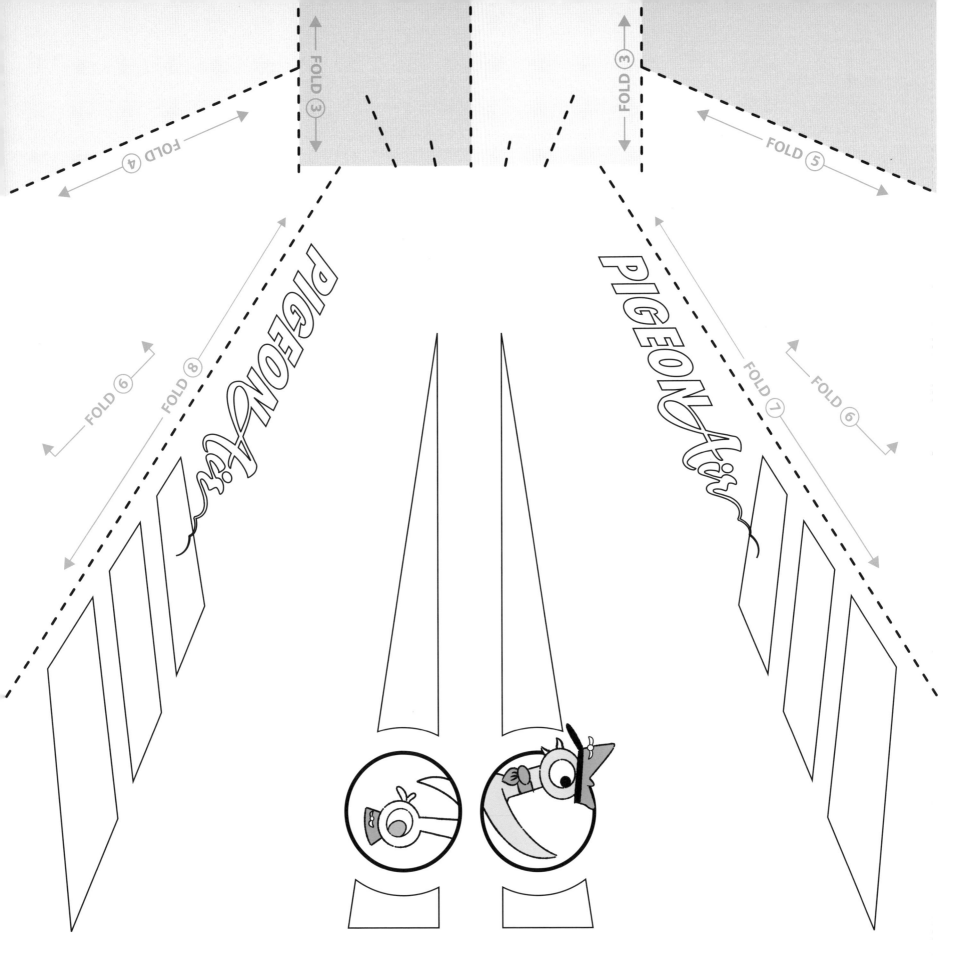

Building an airport!?! That's a BIG ACTIVITY!

1 Pull out the **next six pages** of your activity book.

2 Lay them all out on the table or the floor. Make sure the BLUE side is facing up.

3 Arrange the pieces so they make an awesome poster. It's a puzzle!

4 Tape all of the pieces together.

5 Flip the poster over, and you'll see the Pigeon's airport all ready for you to color!

114

You may want to get a grown-up to help you with a BIG ACTIVITY like this.

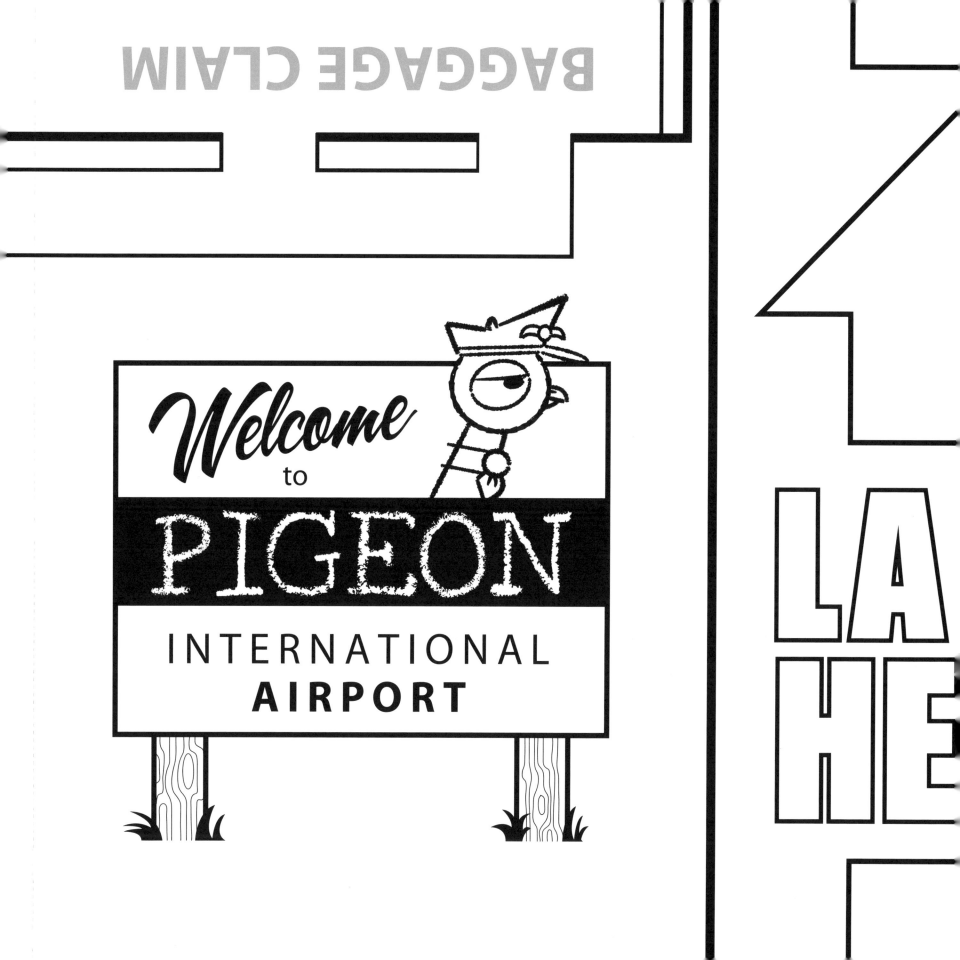

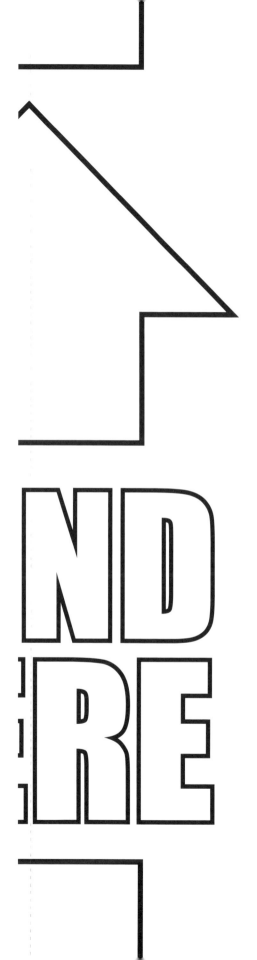

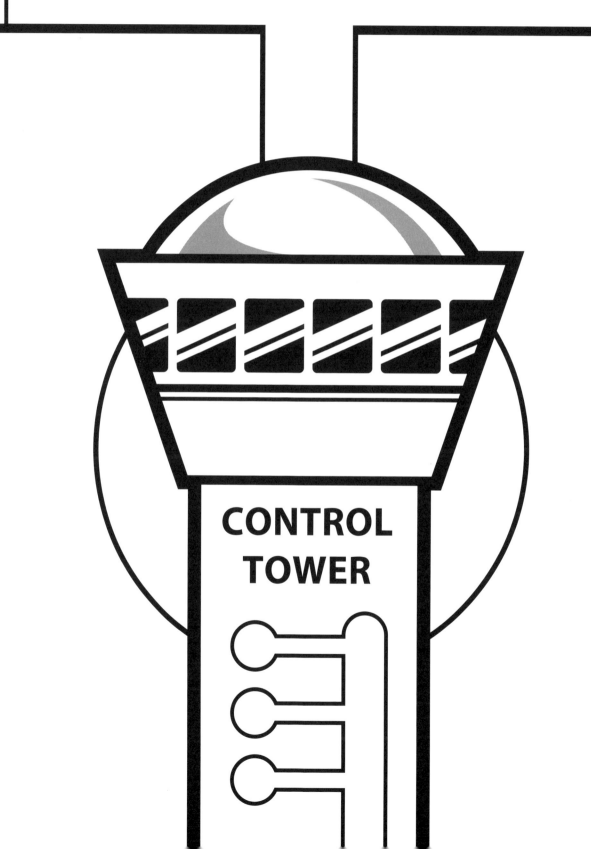

CONTROL
TOWER

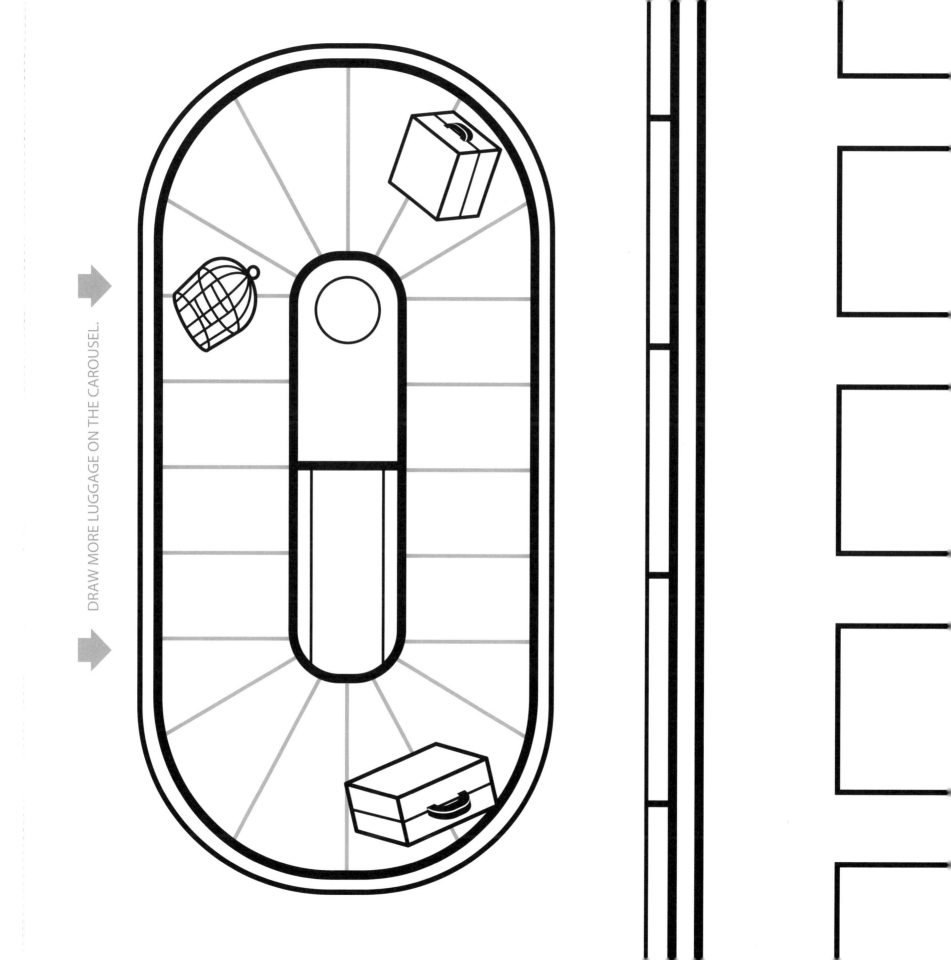

DRAW MORE LUGGAGE ON THE CAROUSEL.

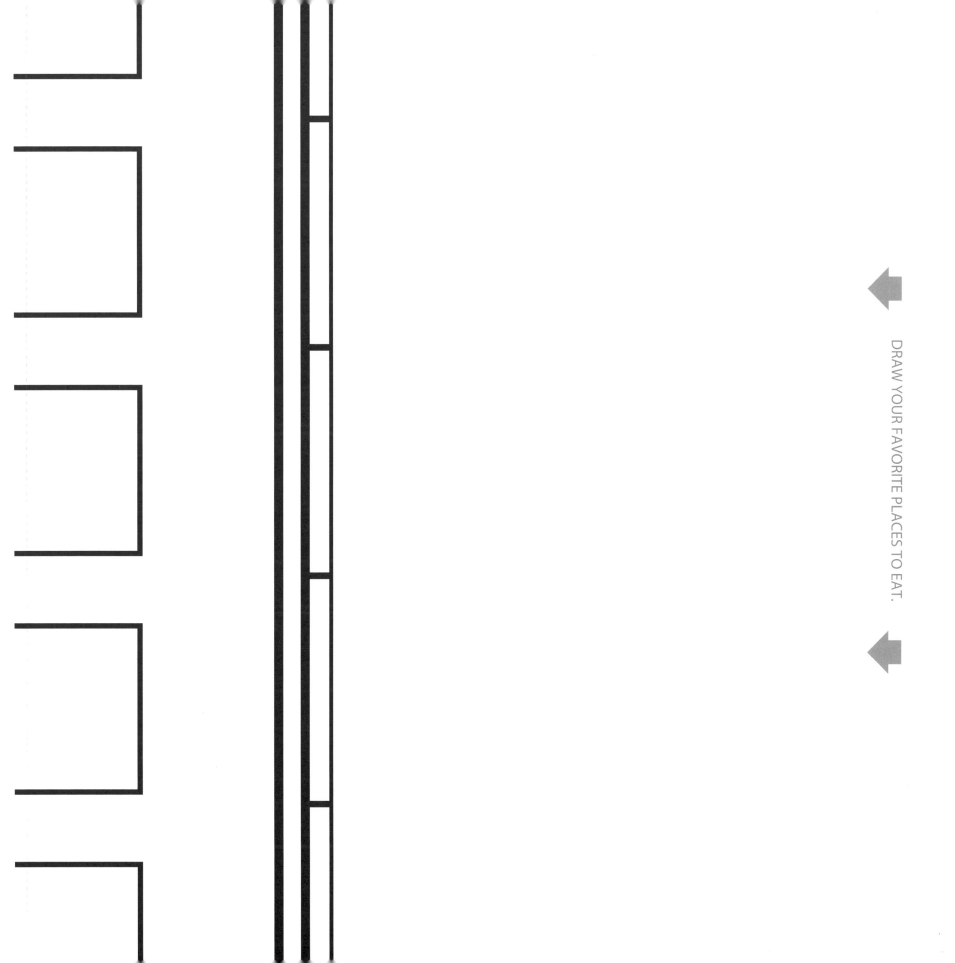

DRAW YOUR FAVORITE PLACES TO EAT.

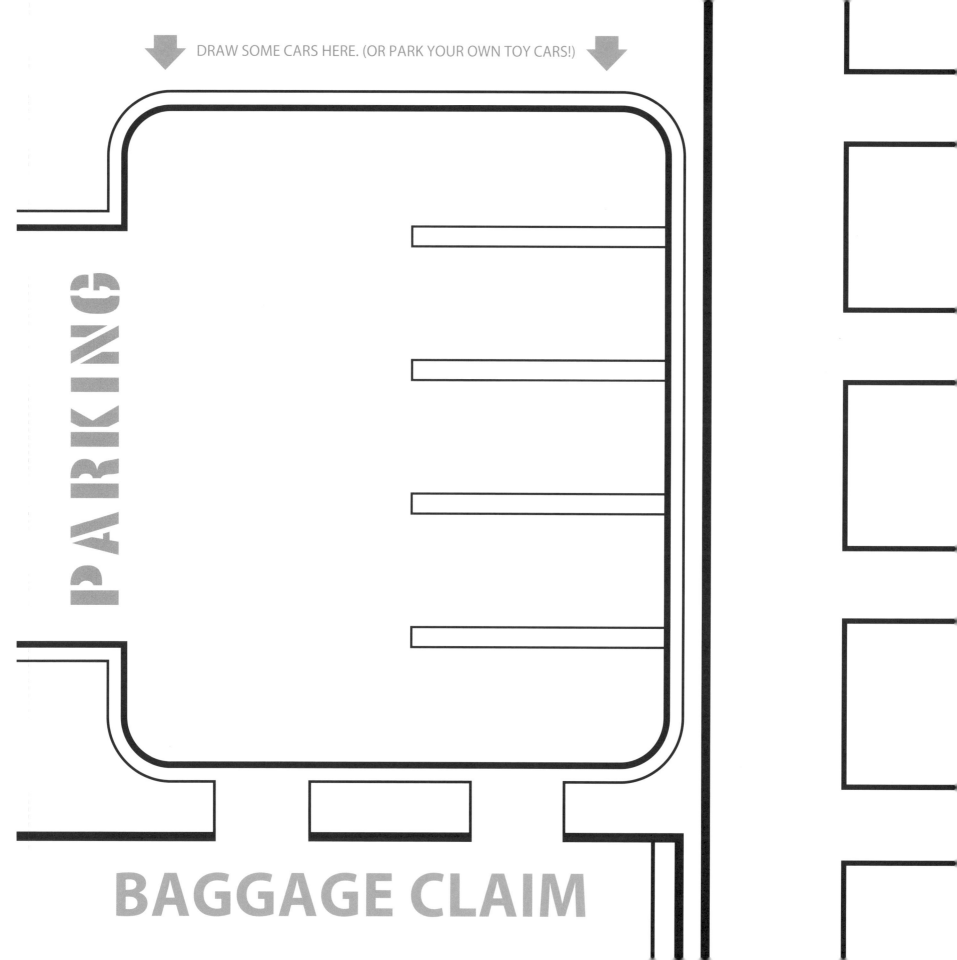

DRAW SOME CARS HERE. (OR PARK YOUR OWN TOY CARS!)

PARKING

BAGGAGE CLAIM

DRAW A HELICOPTER HERE.

HELICOPTERS ONLY

HELICOPTERS ONLY

FOOD COURT

1 Lay your airport on a floor or table.

2 Walk with your airplane to the other side of the room.

3 Try to get your airplane to land on the runway!

You'll need your airplane and the Pigeon's airport for this activity.

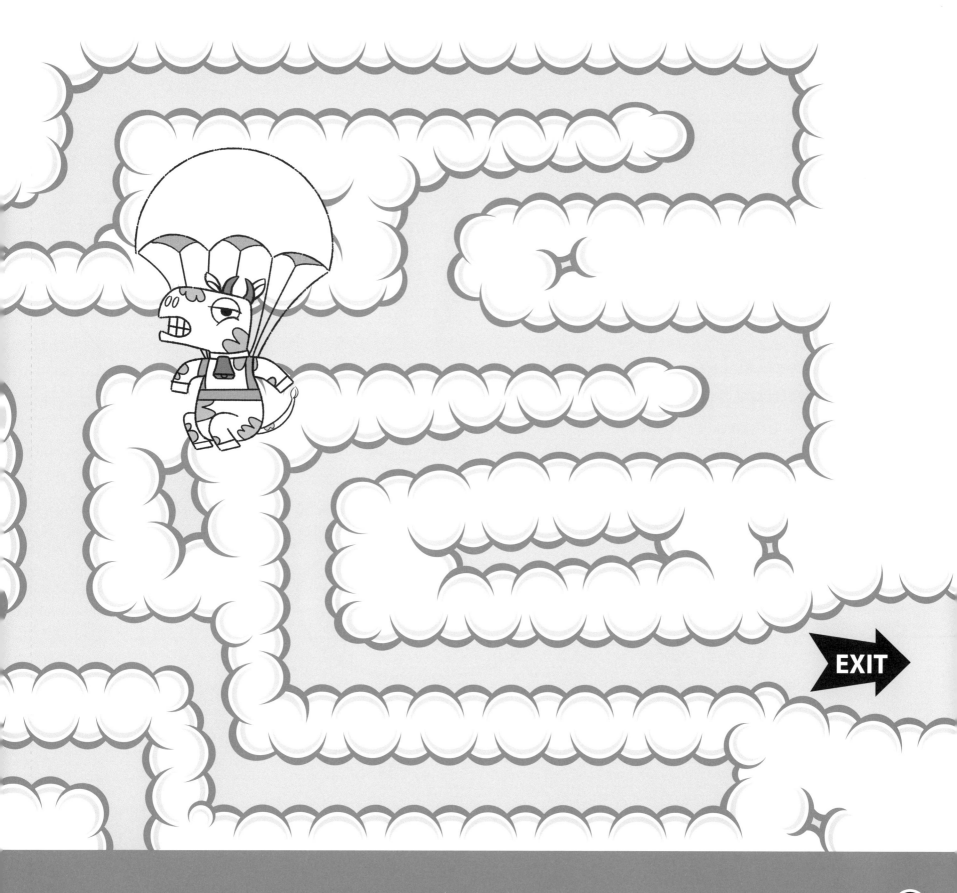

EXIT

Color these two pages with your eyes closed!

THIS is why we're making the puppets!

1	2	3	4	5	6	7	8	9	10	11	12	13
A	B	C	D	E	F	G	H	I	J	K	L	M

14	15	16	17	18	19	20	21	22	23	24	25	26
N	O	P	Q	R	S	T	U	V	W	X	Y	Z

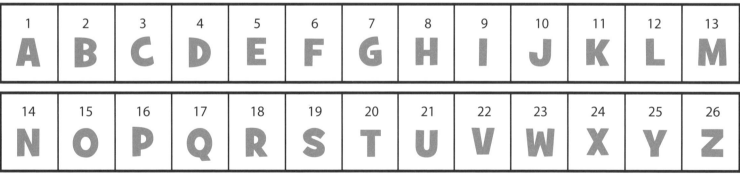

Fill in the blanks using the chart. And if you need help solving the code, the answer is upside down below!

ANSWER: We are going to put on the puppet show!

OKAY!
Let's get this
puppet show
started!

Draw streamers everywhere, and then color this page!

Let's make a Pigeon puppet!

1 Tear out the **next page**.

2 Color the Pigeon finger puppet.

3 Cut along the gray dashed lines to cut out the puppet.

4 Then, cut along the blue dotted lines for the wings.

5 Roll the bottom into a tube.

6 Tape the tube together. It should be a little bigger than your finger.

7 Yay! You just made a finger puppet!

You will need these things to do this activity.

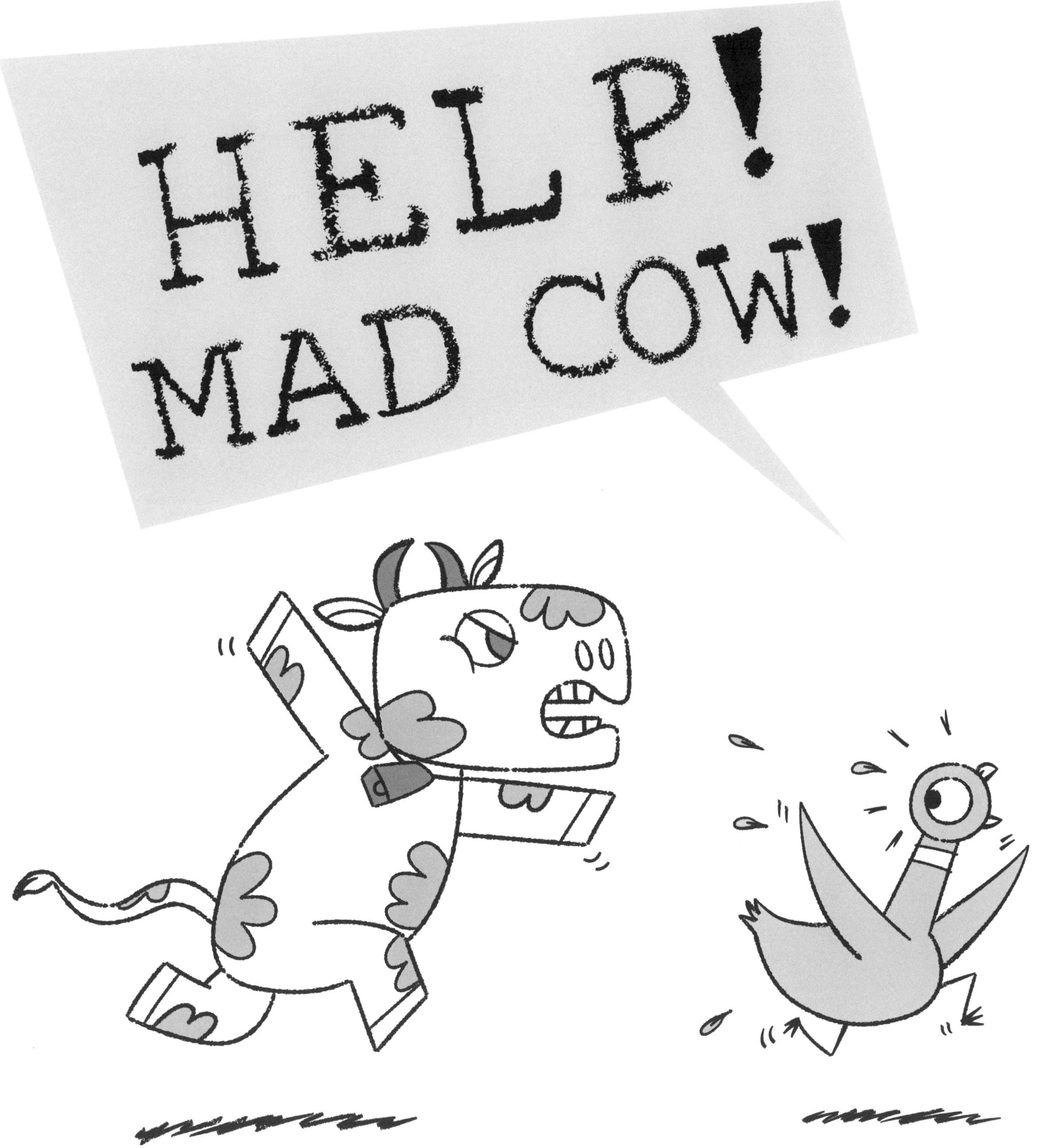
HELP! MAD COW!

Help the Pigeon escape by drawing a path through the woods. Make sure to avoid the trees and broken bridge! But first, color the forest!

140

I made it!

The Mad Cow is chasing the Pigeon through the forest. Draw some trees on these two pages!

Let's make a Mad Cow puppet!

1 Tear out the **next page**.

2 Color the Mad Cow finger puppet.

3 Cut along the gray dashed lines to cut out the puppet.

4 Then, cut along the blue dotted lines for the arms.

5 Roll the bottom into a tube.

6 Tape it together. It should be a little bigger than your finger.

7 Yay! You just made another finger puppet!

You will need these things to do this activity.

144

Draw colorful lines all over the page so it looks like the Pigeon is running fast!

147

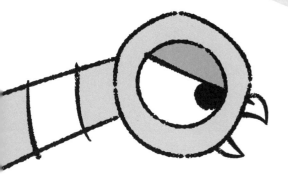

It's time for the puppet show! But where can we do it!?

Color this page and draw party lights everywhere!

149

LET THE PUPPET

To celebrate the start of the show, fill the page with colorful fireworks!

Here's my secret sandwich recipe!

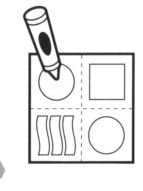

1 Tear out the **next four pages** of the book.

2 Color everything in!

3 Cut out each square.

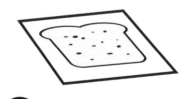

4 Start with a piece of "bread" on the bottom.

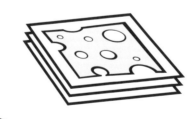

5 Stack up all the different things you like!

6 Put a piece of "bread" on top and . . .

YOU JUST MADE A SANDWICH!

You will need these things to make your sandwich.

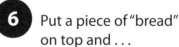

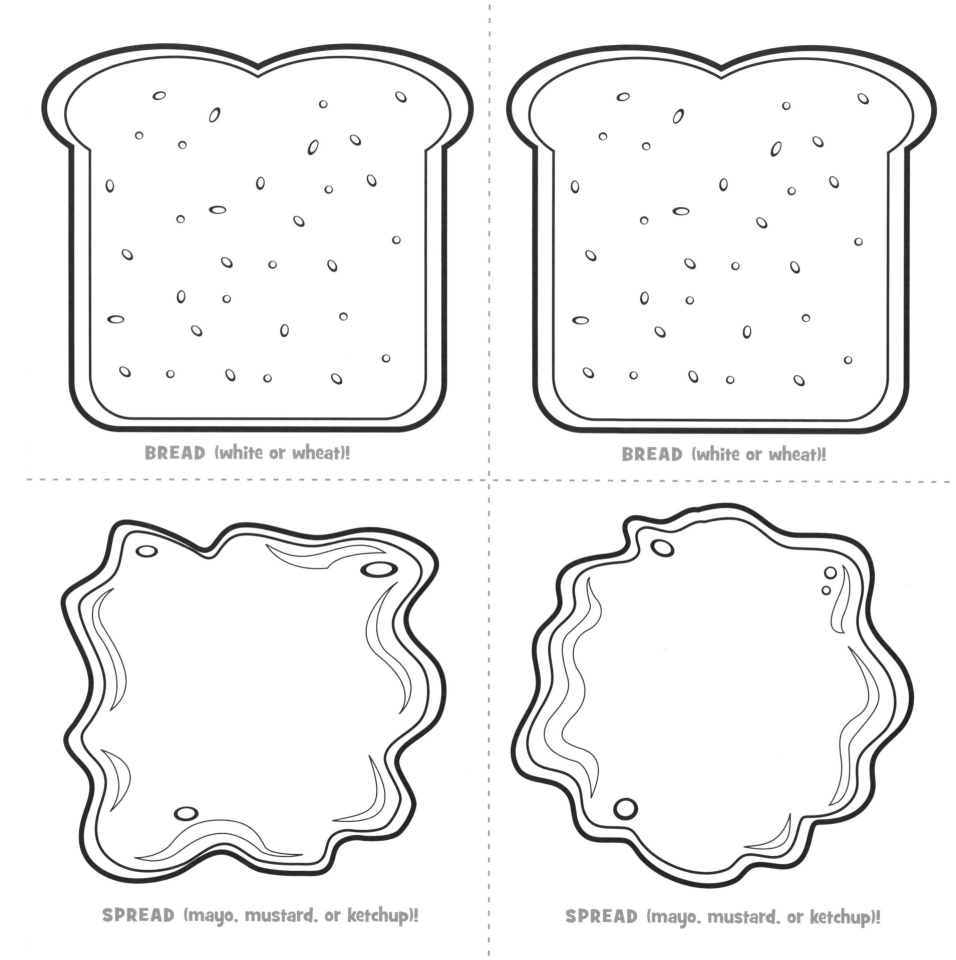

BREAD (white or wheat)!

BREAD (white or wheat)!

SPREAD (mayo, mustard, or ketchup)!

SPREAD (mayo, mustard, or ketchup)!

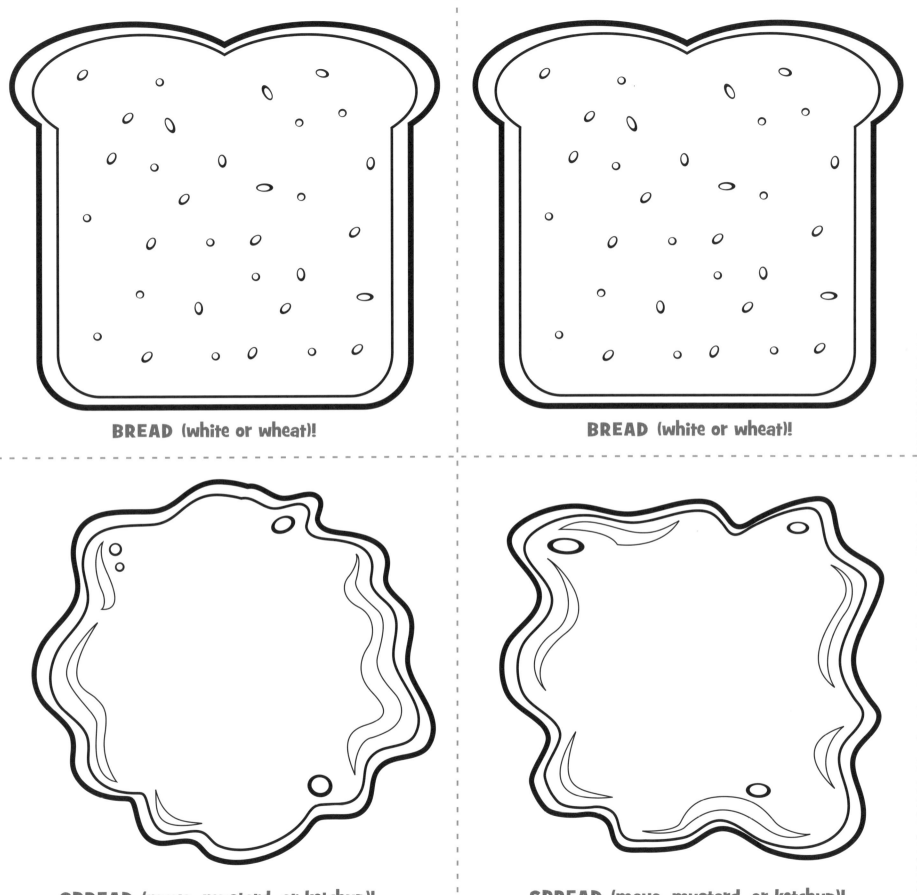

BREAD (white or wheat)!

BREAD (white or wheat)!

SPREAD (mayo, mustard, or ketchup)!

SPREAD (mayo, mustard, or ketchup)!

HAM OR TURKEY!

CHICKEN OR TUNA SALAD!

BACON! BACON! BACON!

A SLICE OF ONION!

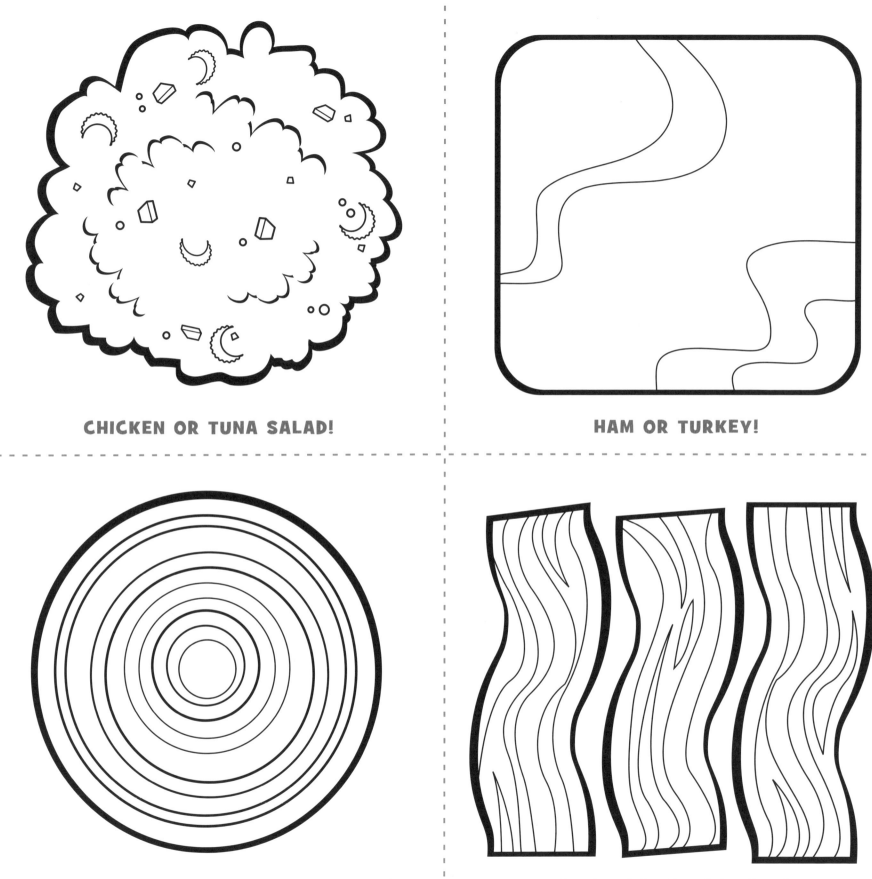

CHICKEN OR TUNA SALAD!

HAM OR TURKEY!

A SLICE OF ONION!

BACON! BACON! BACON!

TOMATOES!

SWISS CHEESE!

LETTUCE!

SOME OTHER KIND OF CHEESE!

SWISS CHEESE!

TOMATOES!

SOME OTHER KIND OF CHEESE!

LETTUCE!

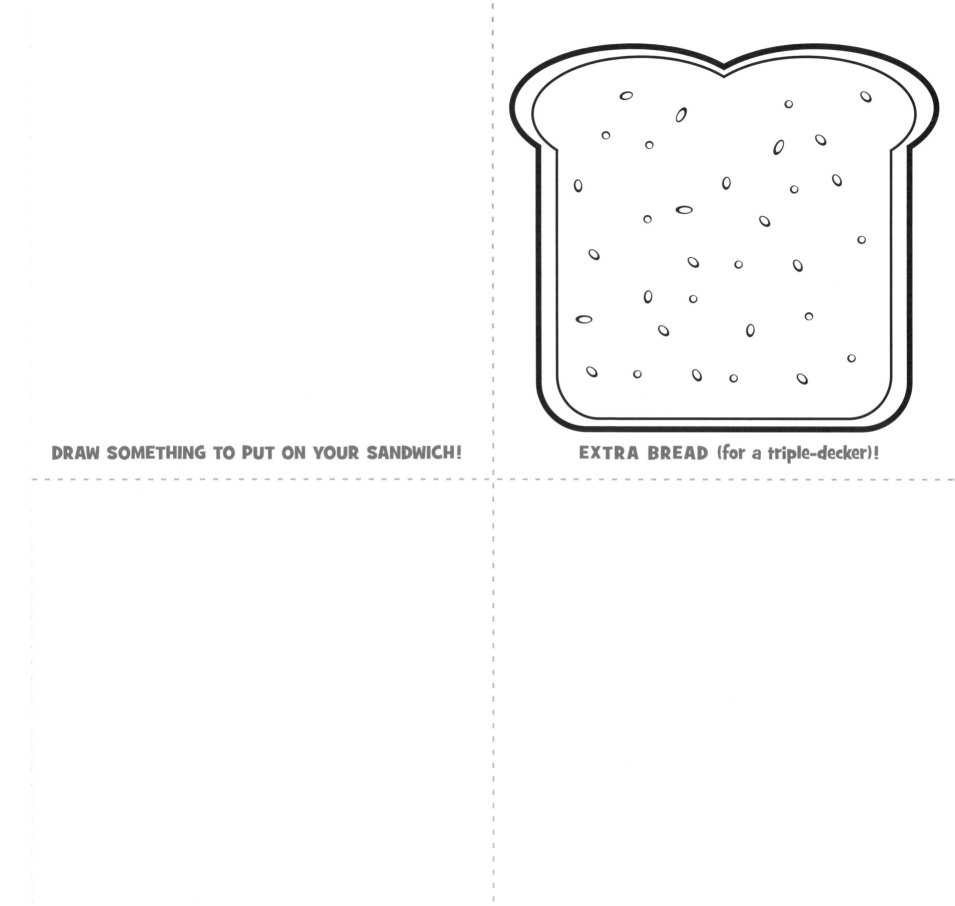

DRAW SOMETHING TO PUT ON YOUR SANDWICH!

EXTRA BREAD (for a triple-decker)!

DRAW SOMETHING TO PUT ON YOUR SANDWICH!

DRAW SOMETHING TO PUT ON YOUR SANDWICH!

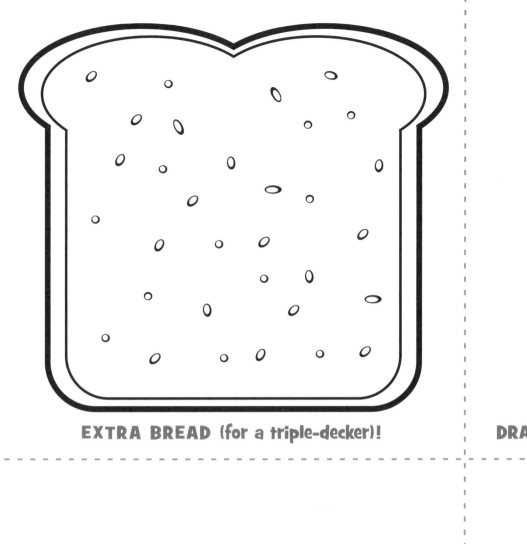

EXTRA BREAD (for a triple-decker)!

DRAW SOMETHING TO PUT ON YOUR SANDWICH!

DRAW SOMETHING TO PUT ON YOUR SANDWICH!

DRAW SOMETHING TO PUT ON YOUR SANDWICH!

HEY!

This sandwich tastes like paper!

166

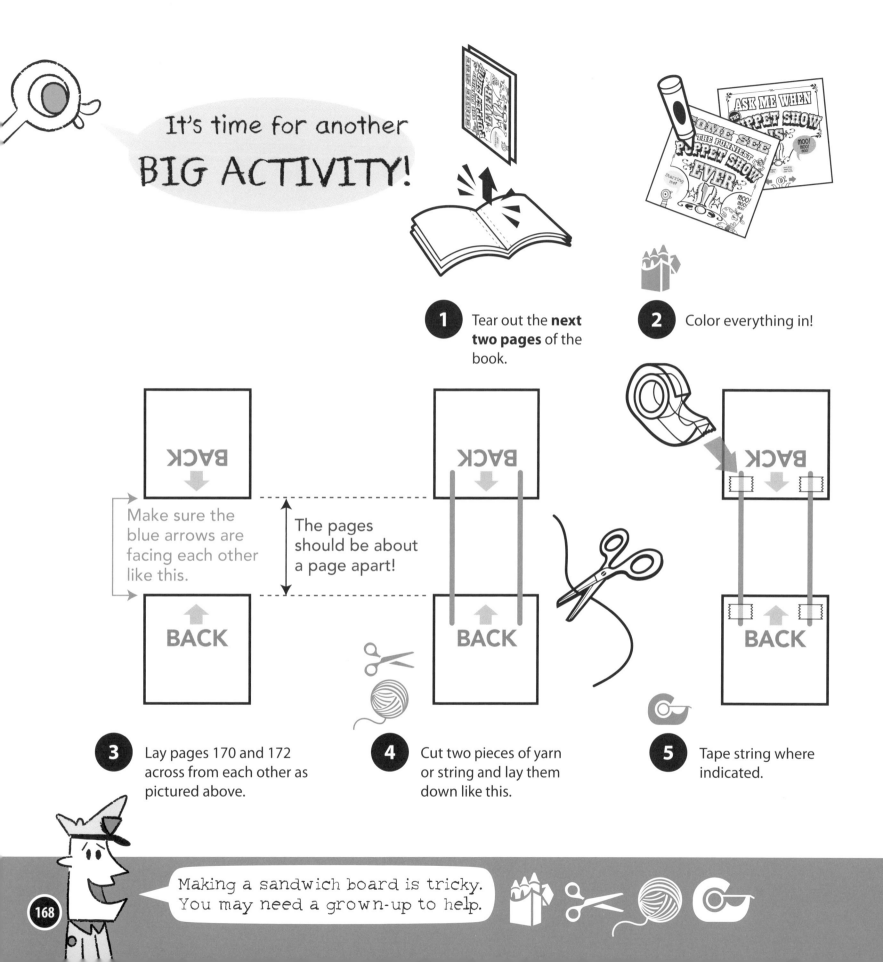

It's time for another **BIG ACTIVITY!**

1 Tear out the **next two pages** of the book.

2 Color everything in!

Make sure the blue arrows are facing each other like this.

The pages should be about a page apart!

3 Lay pages 170 and 172 across from each other as pictured above.

4 Cut two pieces of yarn or string and lay them down like this.

5 Tape string where indicated.

Making a sandwich board is tricky. You may need a grown-up to help.

TAPE HERE

STRING

TAPE HERE

STRING

BACK
OF SANDWICH BOARD

TAPE HERE

STRING

STRING

TAPE HERE

BACK
OF SANDWICH BOARD

When I put the sandwich board over my head, I have a sign in front . . .

and in back!

PUPPET SHOW

Now, let's walk around so people see our signs!

PUPPET SHOW

On these two pages, draw a street for the Pigeon and Duckling to walk on, and then color everything!

WOW! It's another
BIG ACTIVITY!!!

1 Pull out the **next four pages** of your activity book.

2 Lay them all out on the table or the floor. Make sure the BLUE side is facing up, not the WHITE side.

3 Arrange the pieces so they fit together to make a cool poster! (You'll use it later.)

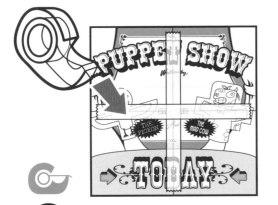

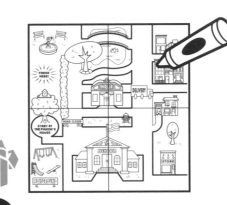

4 Tape all the pages together.

5 Turn the poster over, and then color all the pages of your map!

6 Draw footprints on the map wherever you want to tell people about the puppet show!

 You may want to get a grown-up to help you with a BIG ACTIVITY like this.

FINISH HERE!

PUPPE

Writt

YOUR N

STAR

Draw the Pigeon and Duckling walking through the desert. Make sure to draw the hot sun!

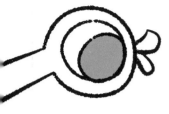

IT'S POSTER TIME!

1 Flip your map back over.

2 Color your poster!

That was easy.
Just how I like it.

 Grab some crayons and color your poster!
And don't forget to fill in any blanks!

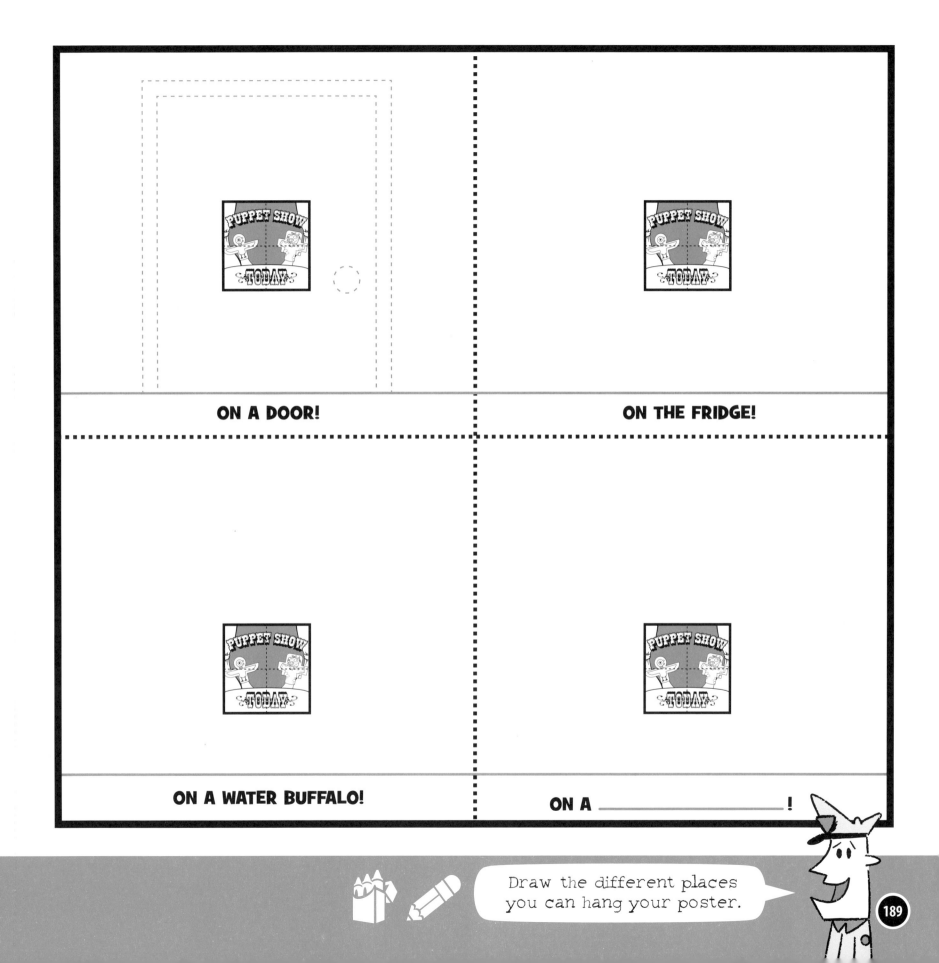

ON A DOOR!

ON THE FRIDGE!

ON A WATER BUFFALO!

ON A _____!

Draw the different places you can hang your poster.

Now all we have to do to finish this activity book is . . .

WRITE THE GREATEST PUPPET SHOW STORY EVER!

THE SCRIPT

1 I am the Pigeon and I want a _____ so BAD NOW!

2 MOO! MOO!! MOO!!!

3 I said I wanted a _____ so BAD NOW. Not MAD COW!

4 MOO?

5 moo! MOO! MOO! moo! moo!

6 moo! moo! moo! AAAHHH! Help! Mad Cow!

Continue chase until you're exhausted or the audience leaves!

THE END!

Help the Pigeon and Duckling finish the story by filling in the blanks. Then, tear this page out and save it for later!

193

START HERE

Help the Pigeon escape the Mad Cow by coloring every square with the Pigeon inside!

FINISH!

I did it!

197

The Pigeon is sweating after all that running around. Draw lots of sweat and big puddles underneath him! Then color these two pages!

Shhhh! The Pigeon is catching some Z's.
How many Z's can you draw on these pages?

200

 Big Z's, little Z's, fat Z's, skinny ones! Draw as many different kinds of Z's as you can!

IT IS TIME FOR

PUPPET

THE SHOW!

Do your puppet show now. Have fun!

After the show is over, come back and tell us how it went!

So . . . how was your puppet show?

CHECK ONE:

☐ AWESOME

☐ REALLY AWESOME

☐ AWESOMELY AWESOME

☐ NOT BAD, BUT I DON'T THINK THE AUDIENCE UNDERSTOOD THE DEEP SYMBOLOGY OF THE NARRATIVE STRUCTURE.

☐ BROADWAY PUPPET THEATER . . . HERE I COME!

Let's make Duckling and Bus Driver puppets!

1 Tear out the **next page**.

2 Color the Duckling finger puppet.

3 Cut along the gray dashed lines to cut out the puppet.

4 Then, cut along the blue dotted lines.

5 Roll the bottom into a tube.

6 Tape it together. It should be a little bigger than your finger.

7 Yay! You just made a finger puppet!

You will need these things to do this activity.

I'd love to be in a puppet show about hot dogs!

Hey! The back of
my puppet is cute, too!

Do you think the Bus Driver will let the Pigeon drive the bus?

Follow the same instructions for the Duckling puppet to make MY puppet!

211

That was a GREAT nap!
Now, let's get this
puppet show started.

Actually,
you missed
the puppet
show.

I MISSED THE PUPPET SHOW!?!

The Pigeon is so upset, his feathers are flying everywhere!
Draw as many feathers as you can on this page!

FREE!

That's news to me!

WEATHER

BEST PUPPET SHOW EVER!

Critics are crazy for the latest puppet show by

_____
YOUR NAME

I laughed so hard that

_____
NOUN

came out of my nose! Everyone

should stop _____ ing
VERB

and go see this show right now!

_____
YOUR NAME

Pigeon Post Reporter

Here's a picture I drew of the best part of the puppet show!

The Pigeon Post

PIGEON MISSES
BEST PUPPET SHOW EVER!

Today a very silly pigeon missed a
great puppet show because _____

_____

_____

_____

_____

Be a reporter and write why
the Pigeon missed the show.

Hey, this is just the front page.

Where's the rest of the newspaper?

Hmmm . . .

It's another big activity...
LET'S MAKE A NEWSPAPER!

1 Tear out the **front page** of the newspaper (page 217) and the **next six pages**.

2 Do all of the activities on all the pages!

3 Then, stack the pages with the front page on top.

4 Staple the pages where indicated.

Oh, boy! We will be finished with this activity book really soon!

You will need these things to make your newspaper!

The Weather Section

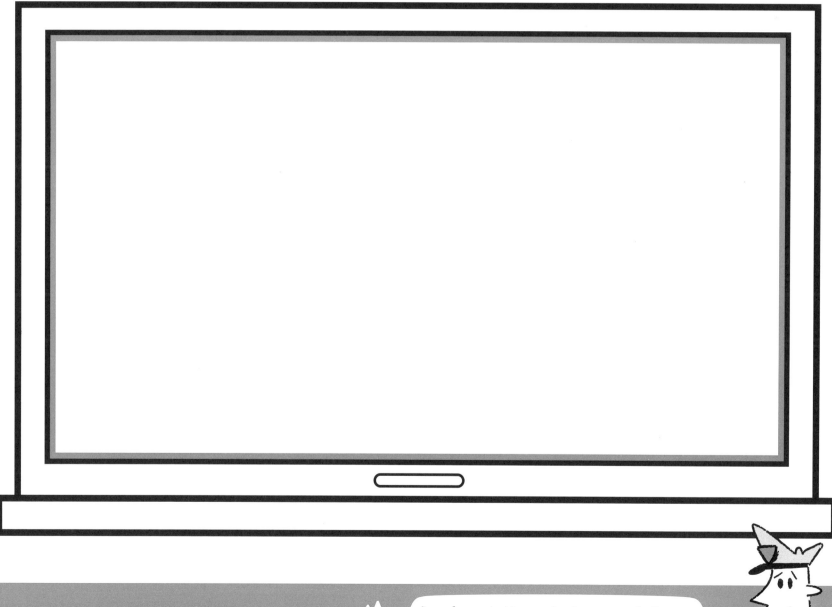

 Look out the window and draw what the weather looks like!

The Pigeon Post

The Arts Section

GREATEST DRAWING EVER
DONATED TO LOCAL MUSEUM!

Everyone jumped up and down and shouted "YAY!" when the latest awesome drawing by

_____
YOUR NAME

was given to a local museum. "As you can see from the image on the next page," said famous art expert Art Artson, "this drawing is the greatest ever.

"I hope everyone will come to our museum to see it and buy postcards at the gift store!"

Draw something awesome in this frame! No pressure.

The Games Section

THE WORLD'S STRONGEST COW?
(OR THE WORLD'S EASIEST CONNECT-THE-DOTS!)

1.

2.

Connect the numbered dots on this page to see the world's strongest cow!

 Pictures **A** and **B** are almost the same.
Circle the 10 differences in picture **B**.

The Pigeon Post

The Good Sports/Bad Sports Section

THE DUCKLING BEATS THE PIGEON AT TENNIS

In the biggest tennis match of the year, the Duckling beat the Pigeon with a score of 2,451 to 2 (and a half). "I've never seen a game like that!" said the umpire. "It's impossible to score that many points in tennis, but that Duckling is so darn cute, I couldn't resist giving her extra points!"

After the match, the Pigeon claimed he lost because he was hungry.

The Pigeon sure missed a lot of balls!
Draw as many as you can on his side of the court.

The Comics Section
(The best part of the newspaper)

PIGEON IS A COW-ARD!

Written by _____

You're the cartoonist! Fill in the empty balloons with words and the blank panels with drawings.

WHAT'S ALL THE BUS ABOUT?

Illustrated by _____

DOG DAY LAUGHTER 'TOON!

Written &
illustrated by _____

Draw more comics!

Title: _____

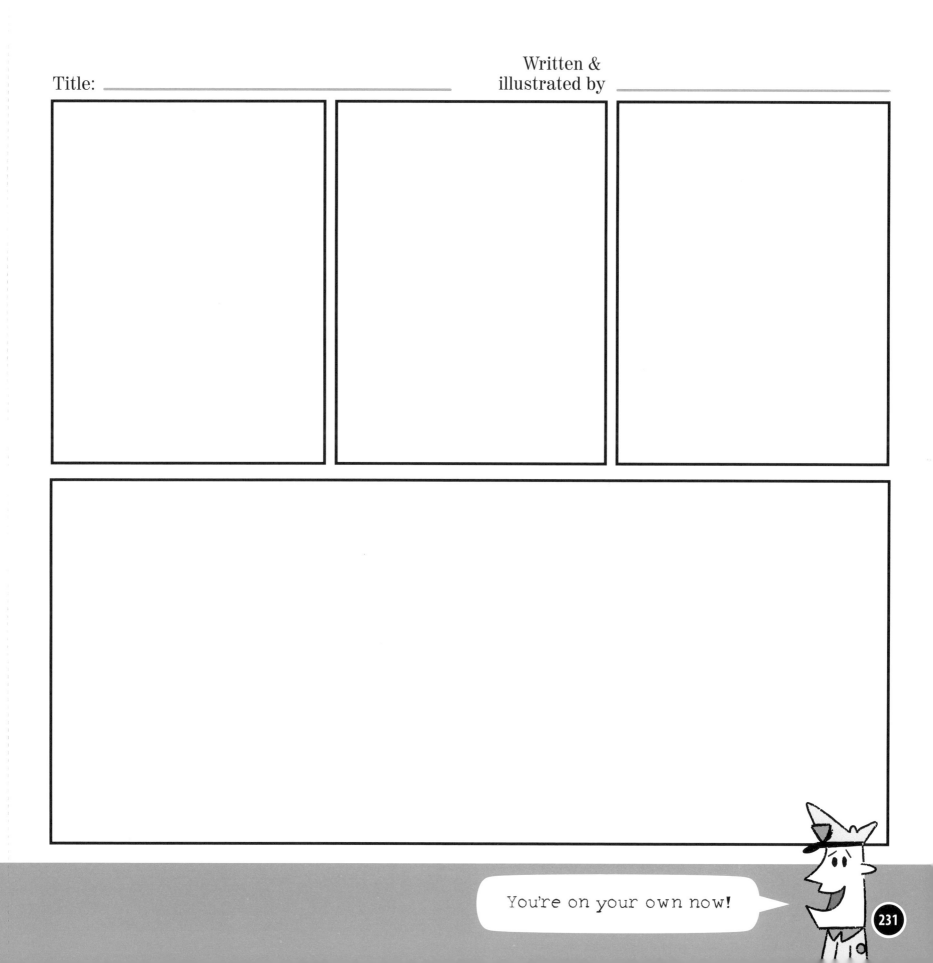

You're on your own now!

The Pigeon Post

The Back Page
(The other best part of the newspaper)

OUR ROVING REPORTER ASKS:
"WHAT IS YOUR FAVORITE FOOD?"

The Pigeon

1. Hot dogs
2.
3.

Mad Cow

1. MOO! MOO! MOO!
2.
3.

Me

1.
2.
3.

You will need something to write with to fill in the blanks. Don't forget to draw yourself!

WE ARE DONE THIS ACTIVITY

236

OH, NO!
It's that
Mad Cow again!
And he's
driving ...

The Pigeon is really scared! Draw something creepy on this page and then color everything with superscary colors!

The Pigeon sure does look confused! Draw as many question marks as you can around his head!

243

PAPER BUS
DRIVER'S LICENSE

NAME: The Pigeon

EYE COLOR: Black

ADDRESS: The Pigeon's Nest
1 Pigeon Way, The Big City, USA

FAVORITE SANDWICH: Yours

PAPER BUS
DRIVER'S LICENSE

NAME: _____

EYE COLOR: _____

ADDRESS: _____
_____

FAVORITE SANDWICH: _____

Tear out this page. Then, fill in your paper bus driver's license and cut it out. Don't forget to draw your picture!

This is the back of your paper bus driver's license! You'll need your license later!

Okay! Let's do one last BIG ACTIVITY!

1 Tear out the **next two pages**.

2 Make sure the BLUE side is facing up.

3 Tape the pages together where indicated.

4 Flip the pages over and color your bus!

5 Flip the pages over again and cut where indicated. The four corner pieces should be discarded.

6 Fold upward on the solid black line as indicated.

7 Tape the four corners where marked.

8 Drive your paper bus . . . but don't forget your license!

This is a BIG ACTIVITY, so get a grown-up to help you!

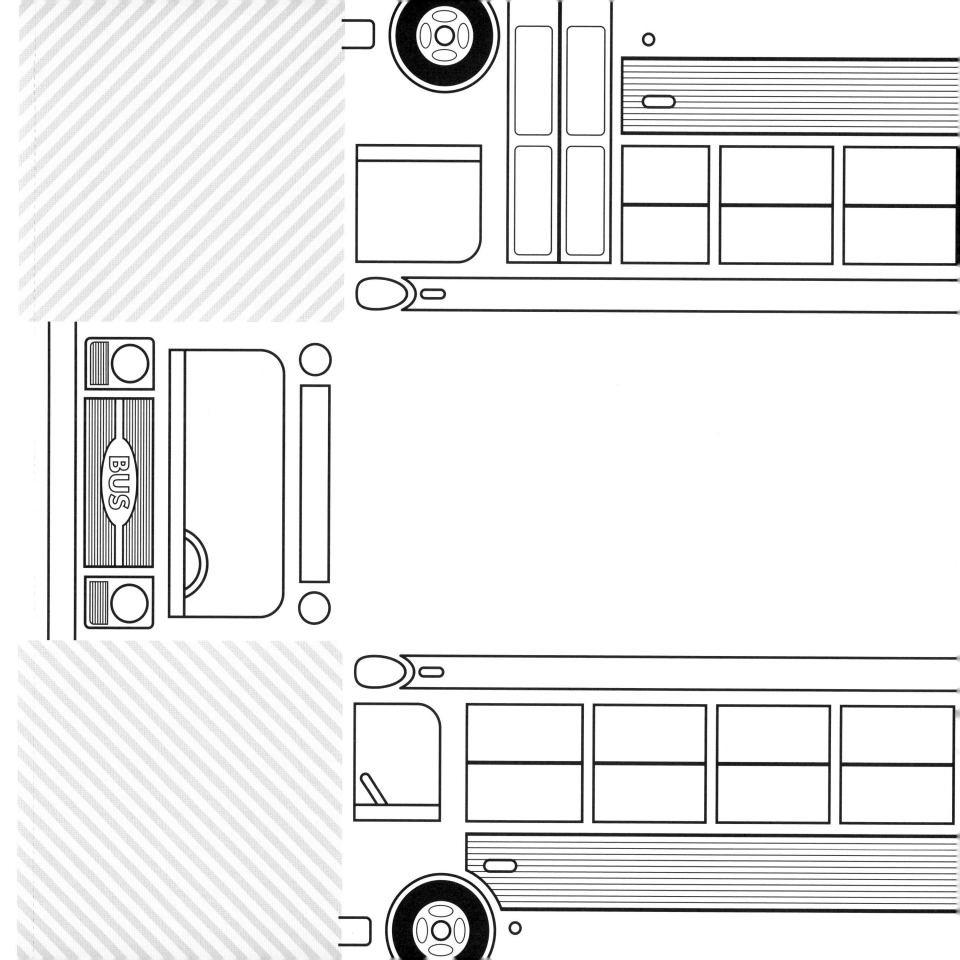

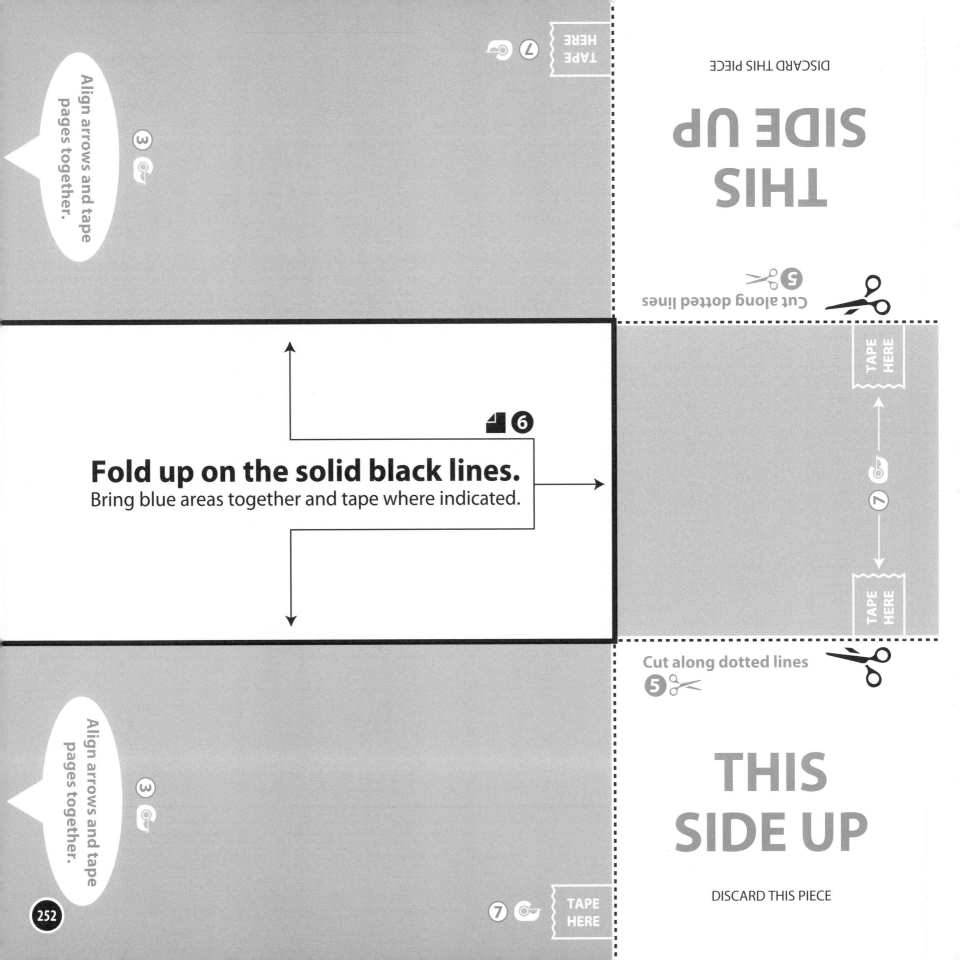

255

BYE!

BYE!

The Pigeon is miserable! Draw rain all over these pages.

The Pigeon is so sad that you should color him blue and put a big messy squiggle over his head!

See you later! But before you go, color these pages as awesomely as you can!

Shhhh... Puzzle Solutions

PAGE 21

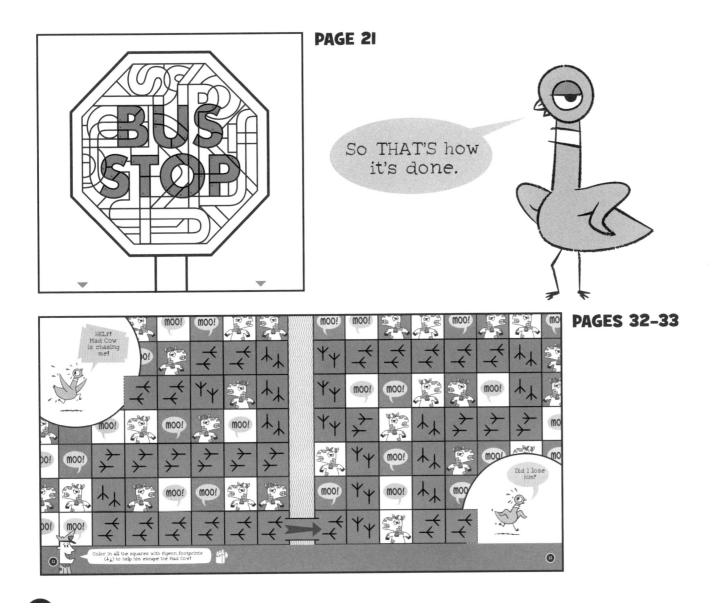

So THAT'S how it's done.

PAGES 32-33

PAGE 40

Who'dah thunk?

"Would you like to come over to my house for a playdate?

The Pigeon"

PAGES 42–43

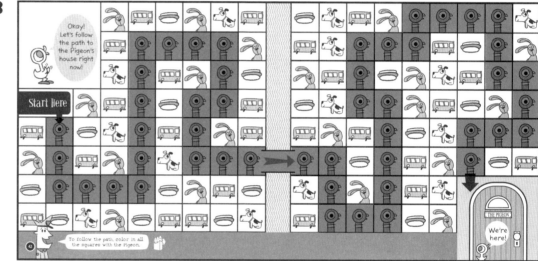

PAGES 54–55

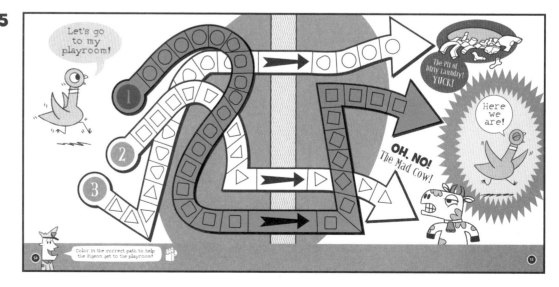

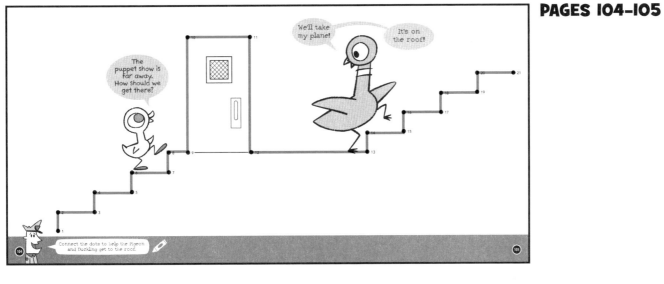

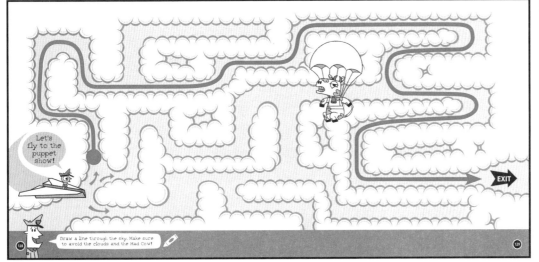

"WE ARE GOING TO PUT ON THE PUPPET SHOW!"

PAGES 140-141

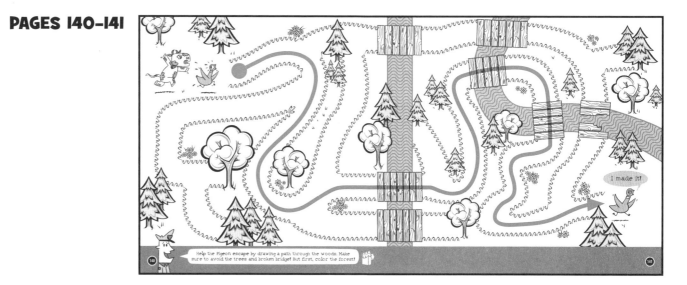

PAGES 196-197

PAGES 224-225

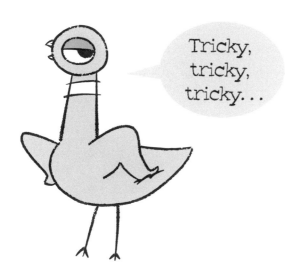